the
Weekend
Crafter®

Decorative Finishes

the Weekend Crafter®

Decorative Finishes

Easy & Elegant Effects for Home Accessories, Walls & Floors

SHEILA ENNIS

LARK BOOKS

A Division of Sterling Publishing Co., Inc.
New York

Editor:

JOANNE O'SULLIVAN

Art Director:

DANA MARGARET IRWIN

COVER DESIGN:

BARBARA ZARETSKY

PHOTOGRAPHY:

EVAN BRACKEN, SANDRA STAMBAUGH

ASSISTANT ART DIRECTOR:

HANNES CHAREN

ILLUSTRATIONS:

ORRIN LUNDGREN

EDITORIAL ASSISTANCE:

VERONIKA ALICE GUNTER, RAIN NEWCOMB, HEATHER SMITH

Dedication

For the Walnut

Library of Congress Cataloging-in-Publication Data

Ennis, Sheila.
    Decorative finishes : easy & elegant effects for walls, floors & home accessories / by Sheila Ennis
        p. cm. — (The weekend crafter)
    Includes index.
    ISBN 1-57990-258-8 (pbk.)
        1. House painting. 2. Furniture painting. 3. Finishes and finishing. I. Title. II. Series.

TT323 .E55 2002
698'.14—dc21

2002016233

10 9 8 7 6 5 4 3 2 1

First Edition

Published by Lark Books, a division of
Sterling Publishing Co., Inc.
387 Park Avenue South, New York, N.Y. 10016

© 2002, Sheila Ennis

Distributed in Canada by Sterling Publishing,
c/o Canadian Manda Group, One Atlantic Ave., Suite 105
Toronto, Ontario, Canada M6K 3E7

Distributed in the U.K. by:
Guild of Master Craftsman Publications Ltd., Castle Place,
166 High Street, Lewes, East Sussex, England
BN7 1XU
Tel: (+ 44) 1273 477374
Fax: (+ 44) 1273 478606
Email: pubs@thegmcgroup.com
Web: www.gmcpublications.com

Distributed in Australia by Capricorn Link (Australia) Pty Ltd., P.O. Box 704, Windsor, NSW
2756 Australia

If you have questions or comments about this book, please contact:
Lark Books, 67 Broadway, Asheville, NC 28801
(828) 253-0467

Printed in China

ISBN 1-57990-258-8

CONTENTS

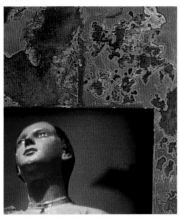

INTRODUCTION

I remember, as a teen-ager, trying to convince my mother to let me paint my bedroom black. We argued back and forth for months until finally we reached a settlement: she would let me paint the doors and wood-work black, but the walls had to remain off-white. Although I felt insulted and artistically compromised, I had to give in. She, after all, paid the bills. But when it was my turn to own the house, you may be certain there was no off-white. Red, orange, purple, even chartreuse, yes. But no off-white. I won't say my rooms were always tasteful, or even bearable, but they were colorful.

I've always been a believer in the power of color. Color does more to transform the atmosphere of a room than any other component—more than furniture, rugs, window treatments, or accessories. Color sets a mood and lets you express yourself. Often overlooked, but just as important as color, is texture. And a good, subtle decorative finish is the perfect way to combine the powers of color and texture, unifying a look and helping everything in the room to make sense.

What is a decorative finish? More than just a paint treatment, a decorative finish takes a surface beyond a flat layer and adds another dimension, making it richer, deeper, and more textured. A faux finish (in which a surface such as marble or wood is simulated with paint and glaze) is one kind of decorative finish, but that's just the beginning. You can use glaze, plaster, stencils, imprints, and embossed borders and more to create an infinite variety of textures.

A good decorative finish makes a room warmer and more personal, or more elegant. It can also take the place of a rug or wallpaper, giving you the flexibility to change your mind and the freedom to choose your own colors and patterns. But decorative finishing isn't just for walls and floors. You can transform unfinished furniture, home accents and accessories, or painted wooden pieces. You aren't limited to working with wooden or plaster surfaces, either. With a little chemistry, you can create a stunning finish on metallic surfaces.

Achieving the sophisticated look you want can seem intimidating. In fact, my first attempt at a decorative finish was an unmitigated disaster. I was trying to replicate a beautiful leathery brown, antiqued finish I had seen in an English pub. My walls ended up looking like chocolate and vanilla swirl pudding rather than leather. After consulting books, taking courses, practicing, and experimenting, I finally got the hang of it. The trick, it turns out, is to know your materials and start small. That's what this book is about.

In the Getting Started section, we begin by discussing the materials and tools you need to create basic finishes. You'll learn about different products available made especially for decorative painting, and discover how easy it is to use everyday household items like plastic bags to create beautiful subtle finishes. Next, you'll learn how to prepare surfaces, from walls to painted furniture, for finishing. I'll introduce you to six basic techniques that can easily be applied to a variety of surfaces. Finally, we'll review some basic facts about color that will help you combine paints and glazes to achieve the best results. The Glossary contains terms that you'll refer to over and over again as you work on the projects.

In the next section of the book, you'll find 20 attractive and functional projects that introduce a variety of techniques and let you practice your skills on a small scale, maximizing your chances for success before moving on to larger projects, like walls. Every finish you'll learn to create can be reproduced on either a wall or an object.

Finally, the Gallery section of the book will provide you with ideas and inspiration for your rooms.

You may not create a perfect finish your first time out, but with just a little patience and practice, you can create a professional look. Relax and remember…it's only paint—you can always paint over it!

GETTING STARTED

Materials

There are hundreds of specialty products available for decorative painting, ranging from expensive single-purpose brushes to metallic glazing powders. Before you sink a lot of money into advanced tools and materials, it's important to familiarize yourself with the basics. To create most simple finishes, all you really need is a base coat of paint, glazing medium and tint, and a simple tool for manipulating the glaze. The following section of the book will introduce you to these materials and others you'll need for a variety of projects. Most of these supplies can be purchased at paint or home improvement stores, although you may find better quality products through online sources. To search online, try using the keywords *faux finish, faux effects, faux finishing schools, faux finish products, glazing medium,* or *Venetian plaster,* and see what you find.

PAINTS AND GLAZES

For years, I worked only with oil-based paints and glazes because they were the best on the market. Despite the mess and difficult cleanup involved in working with these products, oil-based glazes stayed "open" (that is, remained wet and easy to manipulate) longer than any water-based products. Also, oil-based glazes are easily colored using *universal tints* (a highly concentrated type of liquid pigment used by professionals), which are available at any paint store.

Tints

Now I only use water-based products. In the last 10 years, paint manufacturers have developed new water-based paints and glazes which surpass even the best oil-based products in quality. These new products are completely non-toxic, they don't smell bad, and you don't need as much ventilation in the rooms where you use them. Water-based paints and glazes can be manipulated as easily as oil-based products, and best of all, you can clean up your tools and work space with soap and water after you're done, saving you time and hassle.

Almost any paint store carries a line of water-based decorative finishing products, and you can also find them at many big home improvement stores. My favorite products, however, are those developed and sold by faux and decorative finishing schools. There are several excellent product lines out there, and most of them can be found online with a little research.

Primer

If you work with water-based products, primers usually aren't necessary. For example, if you're using a base coat product (see the following description) developed specifically to go under a glazing medium, you won't need to use one. You may need a primer, though, if you want to cover up a particularly grimy wall that's been painted with oil-based paint, or if you're trying to paint a very light color over a dark one. If you're painting a wall with red or a dark color, for example, you might want to use a water-based primer tinted as closely as possible to the base coat color you'll be using. This may save you a little money (primer can be cheaper than base coats). Ask the staff at your paint store for advice and guidance on whether or not your particular project needs a primer.

Base Coat or Undercoat

As the name suggests, a *base coat* or undercoat is the first color of paint you'll use in a decorative finish. Depending on what you're painting, you may use more than one coat of base coat before adding a glaze.

You can create a base coat with regular interior latex house paint in an eggshell finish. For the best results, however, use a product called "base coat" made especially for decorative painting. Base coat looks like regular house paint, and is applied in the same manner, but it's not paint. It's manufactured specifically to work under

Base coat in a variety of colors

a glaze, holding the glaze open for 30 minutes or more. Base coats come in a range of ready-mixed colors, or you can buy them clear, or ready-to-tint (your paint store can custom tint them for you). I recommend using base coat rather than latex paint for particularly large projects, such as painting a whole room. You can usually find base coat at paint or home improvement stores, but again, the best quality products are made by faux and decorative finishing schools, and can be ordered online.

Glazing Medium and Tint

Glazing medium is the material that makes all those marvelous decorative finishes possible. It's the transparent liquid that's mixed with tint and applied over your base coat, then manipulated with any number of creative techniques (see pages 22-24). Oil-based glazing medium has a yellowing effect, but water-based medium goes on clear, even though it appears white in the container.

Adding Tint to Glazing Medium

No matter what products you choose to use, the recipe for mixing a glaze remains the same. Always begin by mixing a small amount of glazing medium with a small amount of tint (I use a disposable container as a mixing bowl). Start with about 2 tablespoons (30 mL) of glazing medium. Add a very small amount of tint to the medium and test the result on white paper or poster board. Remember: when making a glaze you can add tint, but you can't subtract it. If you put in the wrong color or too much of the one you want, you'll have to start over. Always experiment with less color first. Add more tint until you achieve the result you want.

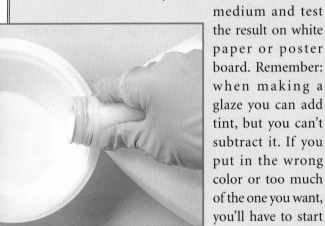

Pouring glazing medium

Adding tint

to start with smaller projects and work up to a wall glazing. If you *only* want to do a wall project, go ahead and give it a try. After all, it's only paint—you can always start over.

Mixing a glaze

The best way to learn about glazing medium is to use it. You may not create a masterpiece the first time out, but once you're familiar with your product, you'll be able to glaze like a pro. It's best

You *must* keep careful notes about the glazes you mix, the base coats you use, the preparation for the project, and any special problems you encounter. I always record on white paper a brush stroke sample of any glaze, along with the formula for the color. These records are *essential* should you ever need to patch and repair a project.

CLEAR FINISHING COAT OR TOPCOAT

A clear finishing coat, often called a *topcoat,* is a coat of varnish or polyurethane applied after the base coat and glaze have been applied and dried to seal the finish and protect it from nicks and scuffs. I rarely use a topcoat on walls that have been treated with a decorative finish. Glazing a wall adds durability to its finish, so there's no need for varnish or polyurethane.

Rag for removing glaze, spray topcoat, brush-on topcoat, bristle brush, roller

Smaller projects, such as furniture, candleholders, floor-cloths—anything that will be handled frequently—do need a protective clear finish like polyurethane.

There are many good clear topcoat products available. They often look milky when wet, but they all dry clear (some oil-based products will leave a yellowish effect). I generally use a water-based polyurethane coat applied with a brush or roller, depending on the size of the project. You can also use a spray polyurethane finish, either water or oil-based. If I'm brushing on a topcoat, I always use a water-based product. It's easier to clean up and just as durable as oil-based topcoat. If I'm spraying a small project, I use spray polyurethane—it doesn't make a differ-ence whether it's water or oil-based because there's no cleanup involved.

When using a clear topcoat, always apply two or three light coats rather than one heavy coat. Polyurethane runs and sags just like paint, so thin coats work best. You may need to sand the surface of your project lightly after the first coat, particularly if you're working with a water-based product.

Clear topcoats come in four sheens, so you'll need to choose a "gloss" that suits your project. A *matte* finish has no gloss at all and is used for finish protection only. A *satin* finish has a light gloss, very little shine, and is perfect for most projects. A *semi-gloss* finish has more shine, and a *gloss* finish is ultra-shiny for when you want a very reflec-tive quality for your work. When it comes right down to it, the topcoat you use is just a matter of personal pref-erence.

CRACKLE MEDIUM

A crackle finish is one of the most popular decorative fin-ishes, especially for furniture. To create an old-paint look, *crackle medium* is applied between two coats of water-based paint. The second coat reacts to the medium, and cracks develop on the surface. In the past, achieving a good crackle finish was unpredictable, quite difficult, and bet-ter left to professionals. Many decorators craved the aged, cracked-paint look a crackle finish gives, but ended up with a messy, muddied surface instead. New crackle medi-ums available today are easy to use. I've had good expe-riences with just about all the crackle mediums on the market, so I buy the least expensive one. Paint stores, art supply stores, and some home improvement stores carry crackle medium.

Even though it's easier than ever to create a crackle fin-ish, it's better to experiment first on small projects, like boxes or furniture. If you want to tackle a large project, such as a wall or a large piece of furniture, or if you want a perfectly consistent crackle, use a sprayer—there sim-ply is no other way to crackle a large surface. Sprayers are available at paint and hardware stores. They're quite expensive, so you'll only want to make the investment if you think you'll be doing lots of spraying in the future.

You should be able to apply a crackle finish successfully by following the manufacturer's instructions, especially regarding drying time between coats. Practice a few times on sample boards before applying the finish to your project. A crackle finish takes some time to master, but is well worth the effort.

ANILINE DYES

Aniline dyes are powdered, synthetic, colorfast dyes that you can mix with either water or rubbing alcohol to use. They're more like stains than paint, and offer great depth of color and absorption. You can find these dyes at art supply and some paint specialty stores. They come in a wide variety of colors and have limitless application. In this book, I used them on unfinished candleholders (see pages 30-31), but they would also work beautifully on cabinetry, furniture, trim, or paneling.

Aniline dyes and paint pens

You'll need to keep a few things in mind when using aniline dyes. First, it takes very little dye to create a deep, rich stain. Don't add too much powder to your mix. Aniline dyes will stain your hands, clothes, or anything they touch, so wear gloves and protect your work surface. Stains from aniline dyes bleed, or seep across and under a surface. If you're using more than one color of aniline dye on a project, don't apply the dyes too close together, as they will bleed into one another.

Always spray on a clear coat of polyurethane if your project uses more than one color of aniline dye. A brush-on clear finish will pick up the dye, and your colors will mix together and become indistinguishable.

DISTRESSING CHEMICALS

Decorative finishes are most often associated with painting on walls or wooden surfaces, but if you want to achieve an interesting effect on a metallic surface, you can use chemicals instead of paint and glaze. Copper, silver, gold, or dutch metal leaf all react to chemical compounds such as sodium sulfate and cupric nitrate, creating unique

Sodium sulfate and cupric nitrate

distressed features. These chemicals are available through chemical supply companies, and most can be purchased online or through catalogues. Buy the smallest quantity of these chemicals as you can! It only takes about 1 tablespoon (15 mL) of chemicals to create ½ cup (120 mL) of liquid.

When using chemicals, follow all manufacturer's instructions carefully. Protect your skin, hands, and eyes against any contact, and always wear chemical-resistant gloves. Experiment before using this technique on a valuable item, as it's not altogether predictable.

METALLIC PAINTS, FOILS, AND LEAF

I use metallic paints and glazes a lot. They're a perfect way to add subtle interest to a finish—they shimmer and shift in different kinds of light. Gilding with gold, silver, or other metallic leafing can create a rich antique look on a surface, turning a plain or unpainted piece into a treasure.

To add metallic highlights to a finish, especially on small projects, I use a paint pen (available at art and craft supply stores) whenever possible. It gives me more control over application than a paintbrush would. For larger pieces, or when broad bands of gold or silver are needed, I use a flat artist's brush to apply water-based metallic paint.

Metallic paint, paint pens, gold and silver leaf

You can find this product at almost all art supply stores and some paint stores.

Oil-based gold and silver leafing paint is also quite versatile, and appropriate for smaller projects such as furniture or decorative accents (it's too pricey for a wall finish). The drawbacks of this kind of paint are that you'll need mineral spirits or paint thinner to clean up after using it, and its drying time can be as much as 24 hours.

Metallic powders (also found in art supply stores or from decorative finishing supply sources) can be added to a paint or glaze for beautiful effects. To add them to paint, just mix the powder in with your paint for your final coat. The powder will appear to change colors in different lights, and add a warm, rich glow to your finish. You can also purchase premixed, exquisitely rich, and vibrant metallic base coats. Some decorative finish supply companies make their own metallic colorants (bronze, gold, silver, copper), which can be added easily to glazing medium.

FINISHING PLASTER

Finishing plaster or *Venetian* plaster is a fairly new product. It's used to create texture on a wall or a smaller project, giving the surface an antiqued look. It's a lot like joint compound or old-fashioned plaster, but it adheres to almost any surface, and is more durable and impervious to stains than those products are. You can find this plaster in some paint or home improvement stores, or through online decorative finishing sources.

I've used finishing plaster on dozens of projects. It makes a great finish for a kitchen because it's so durable and can stand up to the increased wear and tear in such a heavy-traffic room. Color it, glaze it, or even embed cheesecloth in it for wonderful creative looks. You can sand it to a satin finish, leave it rough, or wax it with furniture wax or even car wax for a deep, rich patina. The more plaster you apply, the more ancient and rugged your result will be. My partner and I once applied 13 coats of this plaster on a dining room in New York, then applied car wax and buffed it with a car buffer. The result was magnificent.

You can use regular plasterer's tools, such as a putty knife and trowel, to work with finishing plaster. You'll need to wear gloves when applying it, as it's difficult to remove from your hands. It's also important to clean up your tools and remove any fallen plaster or mistakes from your surface immediately. When this plaster dries, it's almost impossible to remove.

STENCILS AND IMPRINTS

Stencils are an old standby in decorative painting—they've been used for centuries in cultures around the world. Nowadays, you can find thousands of stencils available at art and craft stores, and almost all stencil makers have websites and catalogues with color photos of their products. Some companies specialize in simple designs; others create elaborate, historical patterns that have multiple overlays. Stencil companies also sell stencil-making tools—acrylic stencil sheets and burning and cutting tools for making your own designs.

A variety of stencils

Stencils are great because they allow you to cover a large surface with a pattern, or create a complicated design without having to do it freehand. It's not necessary to buy specialty paints for stenciling. House paint, artists' acrylics, or craft paint all work equally well. Just make sure your paint is thick enough and doesn't run behind or underneath your stencil.

I've stenciled with a special blunt-end brush, a regular bristle brush, a sponge, and a roller. You'll need to experiment with your stencil before you begin a project. It takes a certain light touch to render a clean pattern without runs and seepage. Also, if you're using the same stencil more than once on a project and repositioning it, wipe the excess paint from the back of the stencil before you move it.

You can make your own templates and stencils from plain white poster board so you don't need to spend a lot of time looking for the perfect pattern. I also use it constantly for making sample boards of my finishes (see page 20) and testing colors.

Imprints, which have been introduced more recently to the decorative finishing world, allow you to take a preprinted image or pattern and transfer it to your project, leaving no raised edges. These are great for when you want a more elaborate pattern or image than you think you're capable of painting by hand. For example, if you want to add a decorative image, such as a floral bouquet or a Chinese character, to a piece, you can simply buy an imprint rather than try to recreate the image accurately. For this book, I applied an imprint to a tabletop (see pages 48-49), but they also work beautifully on walls, cabinetry, and smooth floors. Just place the imprint facedown on a smooth flat surface, coat it with a special bonding agent made especially for imprints, and *burnish* (rub) it to the surface. An imprint can only be used once, and since it's relatively expensive, you should follow the manufacturer's directions exactly so that you don't waste your product. You must protect the finish with a topcoat to preserve it.

EMBOSSED WALLPAPER BORDERS

Prepasted, embossed wallpaper borders are an easy, inexpensive, and unique way to decorate your walls. You can use an embossed border at chair-rail height (see project on pages 64-65), at the top or bottom of your wall as a border, or you can even find embossed wallpapers suitable for allover application. These specialty borders are available wherever wallpaper is sold.

When working with a border, you'll need to paint and glaze the paper first, and then hang it. When applying paper to an entire wall, you'll apply the paper first, then paint and glaze it.

TISSUE PAPER

Cheap white tissue, the kind used to wrap presents, can be used to create an interesting leather-like texture (see pages 32-33).

Tools and Equipment

You'll use different tools and equipment for different projects, but the following list outlines the best supplies to have on hand for creating the finishes used in this book.

PREP TOOLS AND SUPPLIES

Drop Cloths

You'll need drop cloths to protect your floors, furniture, and work area while undertaking big projects. For wall painting jobs, you'll need at least one good canvas drop cloth with vinyl backing, and some inexpensive plastic drop cloths that you can throw away when you're done. Drop cloths can be found at hardware and home improvement stores. Even if you get a lot of paint on your canvas drop cloth—don't worry. It will dry and won't interfere with future use.

Putty Knives

A putty knife is a simple flat-edged tool that you'll use for applying filler to holes when preparing a room for painting or for transferring plaster to a trowel for plaster finishes. You can also use it to scrape off old caulking when you're working on a wall.

3-in-One Tool

A 3-in-one tool includes a screwdriver, putty knife, can opener, and more. This useful and versatile tool can be purchased at any hardware store. You'll often use it for removing hardware from furniture, scraping paint and caulking, opening paint cans, and cutting tape.

Hole filler, putty knife, tack cloth, trowel, sandpaper, razor

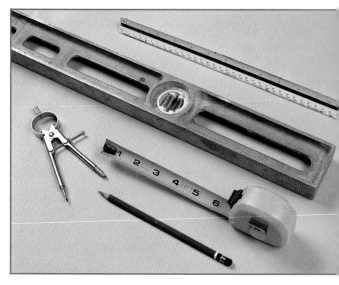

Hard lead pencil, steel measuring tape, compass, level, ruler

Sandpaper (150- and 220-grit)

I use 150-grit sandpaper to smooth out rough spots, and fine-grit (220) to create a perfectly smooth, soft "final" finish. Using a coarser grain may damage a project.

Painter's Tape

You'll need low-tack painter's tape for protecting ceilings, baseboards, or trim from drips and splashes. Low-tack tape doesn't tear the plaster or paint off the walls when you remove it. For some projects, such as the mirror on pages 46-47, use high-tack painter's tape. High-tack tape is stickier, helps prevent seepage, and helps you create a hard boundary—just burnish the edges of the tape to the surface by rubbing them with a coin, or even fine-grit sandpaper.

Steel Tape Measure

A measuring tape is essential, especially for big projects where you're creating patterns on a wall or floor and need to be precise.

Ladder

Get a good sturdy ladder that locks into place. A 5-to-6-foot (1.5 to 1.8 m) ladder is ideal. Try to get a painter's ladder—it has a place for your bucket or roller tray.

Tack Cloth

Tack cloth is just cheesecloth that's been treated with a sticky substance so that it collects and traps dust, dirt, lint, and any other residue that might be lurking on your surface. You'll use tack cloth after you sand to clean dust off your surface before you paint. It's important to have a clean surface before you begin to glaze, because any dirt or dust *will* show up.

Lightweight Hole Filler

You'll often need filler to fill holes and indentations in a wall or other surfaces. Get a quick-drying variety to reduce the time between prepping your walls and starting a finishing project.

Caulk and a Caulk Gun

Caulk is a semi-soft vinyl or rubber product used to seal off the spaces between walls and trim or baseboards, or along windows. A well-caulked seam gives you a smoother surface to work with. Caulking is easy to apply with a caulk gun. Drying times vary between projects, so read your manufacturer's instructions to find out how much time you need.

Bucket of Clean Water

Keep plenty of water on hand for rinsing brushes, cleaning up, and a host of other uses.

Hard Lead Pencils

You'll use hard lead pencils for marking stripes on a wall, creating grids on a surface, tracing templates, or marking off areas that need to be painted. Use number 3 or 4 pencils so your marks will be light and you won't need to erase them. A darker pencil mark is difficult to remove and usually shows through the paint or glaze.

PAINTING TOOLS AND EQUIPMENT
Brushes

You could spend a fortune on brushes for decorative painting. There are dozens of different kinds available, some made only for one specific, limited purpose. I have about 75 paintbrushes, some of which I use frequently, some rarely. Try buying multipurpose brushes to start out with—you'll be able to use them for most finishes in this book. As you become more interested in and skilled at creating finishes, you can add more brushes to your collection.

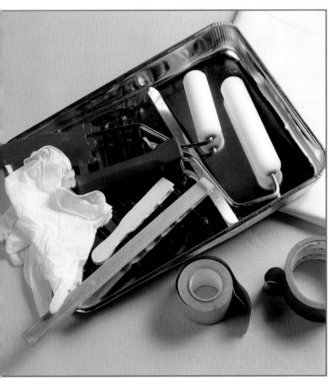

Standard painting supplies

Always buy the best brush you can afford (except where indicated). There really is a substantial difference between a cheap brush and a good one. Cheap brushes lose their bristles, and you'll spend a lot of time picking bristles out of your glaze. The more expensive the brush, the better it will be. Ask your paint or hardware store person for advice. Of course you can use cheap bristle brushes for the smaller projects, but when working on walls, get the good ones.

While you don't need to go out and buy a new specialty brush for each project, there are some basic brushes you'll definitely want to have on hand. Invest in a couple of good brushes for applying glazes, creating *dragged* or *strié*

finishes (see page 22), and applying *colorwashes* (see page 22). These specialty brushes are available at online stores, art stores, and some paint stores.

Bristle Brushes and Synthetic Brushes

I always have one of the following brushes on hand: a 2-inch (5.1 cm) angled synthetic brush for "*cutting in*" (see page 21) and a 4-inch (10.2 cm) synthetic brush for applying glazes and colorwashing.

A *bristle brush* is made from real animal hair or natural fibers. Bristle brushes absorb more paint and hold it longer than synthetic brushes, which are made from acrylic materials. Bristle brushes are great for applying base coat, for pouncing (applying paint with an up-and-down motion for a mottled effect) small areas, for rough blend-

Brushes, left to right: bristle brush, softening or blending brush, angled trim brush, badger blending brush, large bristle brush, dragging brush. Bottom to top: stencil brush, artist's brush, round brush, flat artist's brushes

ing, and even for mixing glazes. They are available everywhere and are really inexpensive. I keep a supply of all sizes on hand. While synthetic brushes are good for applying water-based products, they do not work well with oil-based media. Bristle brushes work with all products, which is why I have so many of them (but I always have a good synthetic angled brush on hand as well).

Artist's Brushes

1-inch (2.5 cm) flat artist's brushes are great for working on small projects and adding details. Get a good quality brush with a fine chiseled edge for best results. You'll also get a lot of use out of a ½-inch (1.3 cm) flat artist's brush. They're great for applying detail and trim to small projects.

Badger Blending Brush

Although quite expensive, this is one tool a serious decorative painter must have. Its delicate bristles allow you to smooth and blend out glazes to a soft, cloud-like consistency (blending is also called *softening* and *dry brushing*). Wipe your blending brush often while you're using it to keep the bristles clean and soft. This brush should be washed extra-thoroughly, as any glaze remaining in the bristles will harden the brush and destroy it.

Dragging Brushes

A *dragging brush*, also called a graining brush, is dragged across the surface of the paint or glaze to create a *strié*, or woodgrain effect. These brushes have long bristles—about 8 inches (20.3 cm)—and are much softer than regular bristle brushes. They are not quite as expensive as badger blending brushes, and can be found in some art supply and paint stores.

Pouncing or Stippling Brushes

A *pouncing brush*, also called a stippling brush, is used for applying paint or glaze to a surface when you want to create a mottled effect with some base coat paint showing through. This brush is also great for getting glaze into corners. Any stiff bristle brush can be used as a pouncing brush; in fact, my favorite pouncer is an old, nearly worn out 3-inch (7.6 cm) brush.

Paint Rollers and Roller Trays

Paint rollers are made of either natural or synthetic material. Natural fiber rollers, such as those made of lamb's wool, are relatively expensive and apply glaze very thickly. I prefer foam rollers—they're easier to clean, cheaper than other rollers, and prevent you from applying too much glaze to an area. I use several sizes of rollers, depending on the project: 4-inch (10.2 cm), 7-inch (17.8 cm), or 10-inch (25.4 cm). Rollers are useful when you're undertaking a big project or don't want to leave brush strokes on your finish. You'll need to purchase a roller frame and an extension pole if you'll be working on a wall,

as well as several replacement rollers. You should also have several roller trays on hand for pouring paint and loading rollers or brushes—the disposable plastic kind make for easy cleanup.

Brushes vs. Rollers

If you're trying to decide whether to apply a glaze with a roller or brush, keep in mind the size of the project and the texture you want for your application. Rolling is faster and often neater than brushing, so if you're trying to be

---

Caring for Your Brushes

If you want your brushes to last, you have to take good care of them. Paint and glaze dry very quickly, and if you put your brush down to take a break, your brush may have hardened by the time you get back. If you don't want to clean your brushes until the end of the project, either put them in water or wrap them in plastic wrap so they'll stay fresh until you need them again.

Always wash your brushes as soon as you're finished with a project. Use warm water and soap, working the soap deep into the bristles. Rinse well and reshape your brush. Tip: For smaller brushes you can shape your brush with soap. After cleaning your brush thoroughly, apply a little soap to the bristles and, with your fingers, smooth the brush to its original shape (pulling all the bristles tightly together so they're not all splayed out). Then simply let the brush dry. The soap remains on the brush and hardens, giving the brush shape; before you use the brush again, simply rinse out the soap.

Dry your brushes first by shaking out excess water and then by rubbing with a soft rag. Either hang your brushes or store them bristle-side up in a container.

To clean an oil-based product out of a brush, swish and soak it in mineral spirits or paint thinner. You can use the same thinner to clean several brushes, but replace it with clean thinner as it becomes muddied. When you've gotten most of the paint out, squeeze the bristles (wearing gloves), then wash the brush with soap and water, and reshape the bristles.

very consistent in your application, use a roller. If you're creating a random, rather uneven application, such as a colorwash, use a brush. I often use a roller just to quickly get the glaze on the wall, and then go over it with a brush to get the desired effect.

Miscellaneous

Keep disposable plastic cups or bowls on hand for mixing glazes and dyes. This cuts down a great deal on cleanup time—when you're done, you can just throw them away. For cleanup, I use a good quality paper rag available by the box at home improvement centers and hardware stores. They can be rinsed and reused to save money.

You'll invariably need scissors for a variety of projects, so keep some on hand. Keep razor blades on hand, too, for scraping paint. You'll also need a level for measuring, and a straightedge or ruler for drawing straight lines (if measurements aren't needed, a paint stirring stick is often a good substitute). When you need a curved, rather than a straight line, you can use a compass, a drafter's tool, to help you get the right proportions.

In addition to their intended purpose, you can use paint stirring sticks for rubbing or burnishing an imprint onto a finish (see projects on pages 48-49). You'll want to have a lot of these on hand for mixing too, so that you don't need to wait for one stick to dry in order to start mixing a second color.

A hair dryer is a great tool for speeding up the drying time on smaller projects. For very small pieces, like the flowerpots on pages 28-29, you can use an oven set to a low temperature for drying.

SPECIAL DECORATIVE FINISHING SUPPLIES

Plastic Bags

Plastic bags (like the ones you get in the grocery store) are great for "breaking up" or manipulating glazes, and for creating sueded techniques (see pages 60-61). Use the thin bags (the thicker ones won't work) and always turn the bag inside out. If you don't, the printed information on the outside of the bag will come off and bleed into your glaze. Refold your bag often or simply wipe it clean from time to time.

Bottom to top: badger blending brush, stencil brush
Left to right: rubber comb, rag, synthetic sponge, sea sponges, cheesecloth, long bristle brush

Synthetic (Closed Cell) Sponges

Large synthetic sponges, available at paint stores, are helpful for projects that include using plaster because the sponge's texture helps smooth it out. These sponges are also great for wiping down walls and removing any chunks of loose plaster before applying your glaze or base coat.

Cheesecloth

Cheesecloth, a lightweight cotton gauze material, is very versatile and useful for decorative painting. You can use it to create a soft, washed finish or to blend out colors in your glazes. You can even embed it into plaster for a great alligator-skin look. Cheesecloth can be purchased at paint or craft stores. Before using your cloth for the first time, put it through the washer and dryer. This gets rid of loose threads and softens it. Cheesecloth is reusable; simply rinse it out after each use.

Rubber Combs

Rubber combs, which create patterns when dragged through wet paint or glaze, are among the most popular and useful tools in decorative painting. There are many different types of combs available in paint stores and through decorative finishing suppliers. Some, like the ones I use, are triangular and have different spacing between the teeth on each side of the triangle, so you can achieve several different effects with the same comb.

Simply hold your comb at various angles while dragging it through the glaze and you'll discover how versatile this tool can be. Remember to wipe off your comb after each drag, or your glaze will "puddle" on your work.

Sea Sponges

Sea sponges are great for applying washes and glazes, for creating a dabbed effect, for blending and smoothing out brush strokes, and removing glaze or paint from a surface. They can create a very random, organic-quality texture. On the other hand, if not done properly, sponging can look very amateurish, very obviously "sponged." I use sea sponges mostly on small projects when I want to introduce some broken color.

You can find sea sponges at art supply or paint stores. They are often used for applying glazes and paints, especially on small projects.

Techniques

Now that you have all your supplies assembled, you're almost ready to start the real work and fun of creating decorative finishes. Before you begin, however, take a few steps of preparations to ensure that you get the best possible results.

PREPARATION

I'm of the opinion that any surface can be painted! Many decorative finishes don't require a lot of prep work because the little flaws and irregularities in the walls often enhance

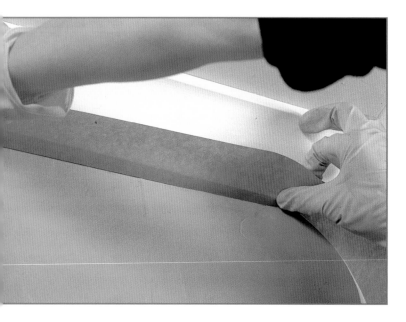

the look—you don't need to aim for perfection. However, for most projects, you'll need to spend some time setting up before beginning a project.

First, gather all the materials you'll need to complete the job. Here's a good general checklist for prepping a variety of surfaces:

Drop cloths (plastic and canvas)
Disposable gloves
Ladder
Low-tack painter's tape
Screwdriver (to remove switchplates)
Putty knife
Hole filler
150- and 220-grit sandpaper
Tack cloth
High-grade vinyl caulk and caulking gun
Trisodium phosphate cleaner*
Bucket of clean water
Clean rags
Roller pan and roller
Trim brush for cutting in (see page 20)
Primer (optional)
Bristle brush (optional)

*available at hardware stores

Preparing a Room for Decorative Finishes

It's essential to protect your floors, furniture, and valuables before beginning to work. Remove as much from your room as possible. Move all remaining furniture and rugs to the center of the room and cover them with plastic drop cloths to protect them from splatters and spills. Be sure to leave enough room around the walls so you can maneuver your ladder.

Cover the floors with vinyl-backed canvas drop cloths. I often tape the cloths around the room's perimeter; this helps keep the cloths in place.

Remove your switchplates and outlet covers with a screwdriver, unless you want to paint them, too (which I routinely do).

Tape off the baseboards, trim around windows, doors, and the ceiling with low-tack painter's tape (see photo left). Use at least 2-inch (5.1 cm) tape on the ceiling.

If you want your walls to be smooth and unblemished, scrape any peeling paint off the walls with a putty knife. Fill holes and cracks with quick-drying hole filler and a putty knife. Allow these areas to dry, and then sand the patches with 220-grit sandpaper (see photos, right). Remove any dust with tack cloth.

If you're going for a very textured look, you can skip the previous step. I generally patch only big holes or unsightly spots, then sand the places lightly so they blend into the walls. If there are small imperfections, I usually leave them (they actually can make decorative finishes look better). If I'm using finishing plaster (see page 11), I never patch—the plaster covers the imperfections, even the holes.

If there is damaged caulking, repair it. Using a putty knife, remove as much of the damaged caulking as you can. Re-caulk using a high-grade vinyl caulk and a caulk gun.

If walls are grimy (as kitchen walls often are), consider washing the walls with a trisodium phosphate substitute and then rinsing with water. This cleaner is available at paint and hardware stores. Allow the area to dry before painting.

Finally, clean your baseboards of any dust. If you don't, this dust will end up in your paint and/or glaze. Since base coats are excellent primers for most walls, you usually won't need to apply a primer before beginning to paint.

Preparing Unfinished Wood for Finishing

First, remove any hardware such as knobs or hinges. Unfinished furniture and decorative pieces (such as boxes, candleholders, or lamp bases) usually need only a light sanding before you begin a finish. If your piece is particularly rough, sand it first with a 150-grit sandpaper, then finish with 220-grit. The surface should be smooth to the touch. If, however, there are rough-cut patches on the piece, fill these areas with lightweight hole filler using a putty knife, then proceed with sanding.

If you're using a latex paint for your base coat, you'll need to prime the piece first. If you are painting your piece with a base coat product (as opposed to a latex paint), you do *not* need to prime it.

Whether you use latex paint or base coat, you will need to sand lightly between coats because water-based products will raise the grain of the wood. When you've finished sanding, use a tack cloth to remove all dust.

Preparing Painted Pieces

If you're putting a decorative finish on an old, already-painted piece, you must prepare the surface to accept new paint. You don't need to strip it unless you really want to—adding layers usually just improves the effect.

Scrape any peeling paint from the piece with a putty knife. Patch cracks or holes (if you like) with lightweight hole filler. Sand the piece lightly using 150-grit sandpaper—this will break up the old paint and allow the new finish to adhere. Remove any dust with tack cloth.

DECIDING ON A FINISH

Now you're ready to start, but how do you decide what finish you want for your project? Decorative finishes add depth, interest, texture, and personality to plain painted walls, but your walls shouldn't be the focal point of the room. You don't want to walk into a room and exclaim "Whoa! A decorative finish!" Rather, you're looking for a feeling of charm and sophistication, and a polished look. If a finish is done correctly, you'll notice only later that it brings all the elements of a room together.

Consider a decorative finish as a carefully chosen backdrop to everything else in the room. What I always tell my clients is this: understate it. Sometimes my finishes are so subtle that you have to get fairly close to even see them, but from a distance they have the desired effect: they're rich, vibrant, organic, and *not* flat.

Okay, so sometimes we go completely in the other direction—the finish *is* the main feature of the room. In small powder rooms, I have created powerful, dramatic, metallic effects that basically do all the decorating work for that space. Once on a long, curved foyer wall, I applied a raised, corduroy-looking metallic finish that was positively stunning. In each case, the client wanted the wall to do all the work. In each case, nothing else, except the floor, was even considered.

Most times you're working with fabric, furniture, light fixtures, rugs, pillows, window treatments, and adjacent rooms, so be careful not to overdo it. That's what makes an amateur effort look amateur.

BEFORE YOU BEGIN: MAKING A SAMPLE BOARD

I always make up a sample board before starting any finish. I apply the finish to poster board first because it's cheap and easy to find. I paint the undercoat or base coat first, then make up a small amount of glaze and apply it just like it's going on a wall. I then tape the board up in the room where the finish is going to go. I (or my client) can look at the board in all different types of light at different times of day. I've made sample boards that look one color in my studio and look completely different in a client's home. A sample board is the only way to be sure that you're getting the color right before committing to an entire wall finish.

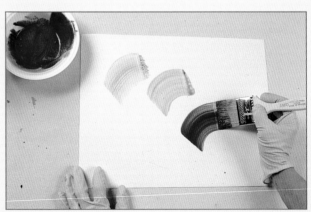

Always try out your glaze on posterboard before applying it to a wall. Add a small amount of tint at a time, testing the color each time by brushing it on the board and comparing the results.

DO THE MATH: CALCULATING HOW MUCH PAINT OR GLAZE YOU'LL NEED

Before starting out on a project, you'll want to make sure you have enough paint or glaze on hand to finish the job. As a general rule, 1 gallon (3.8 L) of paint covers 300 to 400 square feet (27 to 36 m2). I always calculate about ½ gallon (1.9 L) of glaze for a 12 x 12-foot (3.6 x 3.6 m) area. It's better to make too much glaze on your first attempt than to make too little and then try to match your first glaze exactly. I always save a little glaze in a tightly sealed glass jar in case I need a touch-up down the line (see section below).

PAINTING A WALL—CUTTING IN

Before you get out your roller, the first step in painting a wall is "cutting in," or painting the areas around trim, doors, and windows first. Cutting in is done to make sure that these areas are painted accurately without getting any paint on the trim. To cut in, first tape off all the trim and the ceiling. Using a brush, start to paint in the area around the tape, moving the brush out towards the center of the wall. Flex the brush bristles to give it a hard edge, pulling it along the edge of the tape (see photos). NOTE: When I'm simply applying a base coat, I don't cut in—I just paint carefully. I usually only tape off the trim when I'm working with the glaze. If you leave tape on the trim or ceiling for too long, it can adhere stubbornly to your trim and peel off the paint when you remove it. So if you're using painter's tape, get the low-tack kind and save yourself lots of touch-up time.

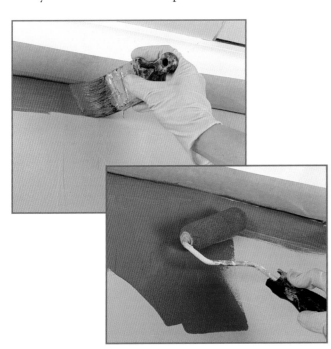

APPLYING A BASE COAT

Unless you'll be applying a plaster finish, apply two coats of base coat or paint. If you're using a dark color, like purple, you may need to use three coats. Red is the most difficult base color to apply; sometimes it will take three to four coats for adequate coverage (this is because red pigment does not suspend well in any medium—just a little artist's fact of life). Always remember: whatever your base coat looks like, it will show through your glaze. Glaze is semitransparent!

GLAZING A ROOM

When you're applying glaze to all the walls in a room, look for logical places to stop and start. Once you start glazing, you can't stop in the middle of a wall. Be sure to mix enough glaze to finish the project; you won't have time to take a break to mix more glaze. Read the label on the glazing medium container to find out how much wall space the product will cover. This isn't an exact science, as you may need more glaze for one finish than others, but it will give you a ballpark figure. Always make more than you think you need.

When applying the glaze, create a random edge, that is, do not apply your glaze in straight sections or squares, but rather apply it in loose, organic patterns. You don't want your walls to appear to be paneled.

Also, you must keep a wet edge. This means you don't manipulate your glaze all the way to the edge of your application—leave about a 4 to 6-inch (10.2 to 15.2 cm) area that is not manipulated. Then, when you apply glaze to the next section, you can work the wet glaze from the previous application into the new wet glaze, and you won't leave a hard line. This technique takes practice!

The best way to glaze a room successfully is to get help. One person can apply the glaze, making sure that the edges don't dry out, while the second person manipulates the glaze. For very large areas (big rooms with high ceilings), it may take three or four people to keep the process going.

SAVING GLAZES

If you have any leftover glaze and wish to store it, put it in an airtight bucket or jar and label it. I try to keep the glazes I use on my house in case I need to touch up or repair. But beware: glazes only keep about a year, maybe less. After that they break down and should be discarded—another reason to take careful notes should you have to patch.

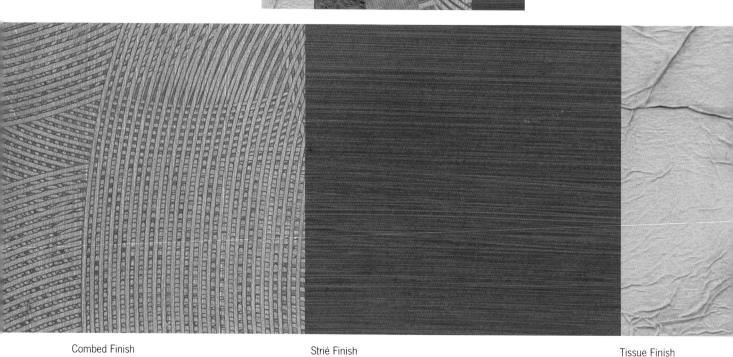

Combed Finish

Strié Finish

Tissue Finish

Basic Finishes

After you've created your glaze and applied it to your surface, the real art of decorative finishing begins—manipulating the glaze to create a textured effect.

COMBING

Combing can create a myriad of patterns—plaid, random crossings, waves—depending on effect the you want.
To create the finish on the sample board above, I applied two coats of off-white base coat and let it dry. Next, I mixed a glaze with dark brown tint at a 1:5 medium-to-tint ratio. While the glaze was still very wet, I used a rubber combing tool to create a random pattern, overlapping my comb strokes so there were no "nonworked" spaces. I then allowed the glaze to dry. For the second glaze with bronze tint, I mixed a glaze at a 2:1 medium-to-tint ratio. I applied the glaze evenly with a foam roller, then brushed out any uneven areas with a large badger blending brush for an overall washed effect.

When combing a wall, you will need to work in sections, always leaving a wet edge as you go (see glossary on page 78). Combing corners can be tricky. Usually I cut a few teeth from the corner of the comb itself, thus allowing me to squeeze my comb into tight corners.

STRIÉ

A *strié* finish creates a dragged or woodgrain effect. To create a nice, even strié takes some practice, but luckily, you're not going for perfectly straight lines, just regular and neat ones.

To create this finish, I applied two coats of basic red base coat (clear red, not warm red). I then mixed a glaze with white tint at a 3:1 medium-to-tint ratio and applied it over the entire wall. The next step is to fold cheesecloth into a pad, and pat or dab the glaze until you have a smooth, overall wash. After the first glaze was dry, I mixed a second glaze using clear red and blue-red tints at a 3:1 medium-to-tint ratio (very heavy). I applied this glaze to the wall with a stiff 4-inch (10.2 cm) bristle brush. Beginning at the ceiling, I pulled the brush down the wall as evenly as possible (at the baseboard, you may have to pull your stroke up from the bottom, blending into the lines you have just pulled down to give you a nice even finish at the top and bottom of your pull). While "working" this glaze, it's important to leave a wet, unworked edge as you go, so you don't create a paneled look.

COLORWASH

Colorwashing is a fairly simple technique. The overall look is what the name implies—the wall looks as if it's been washed with color. This does not imply that it will

Colorwash Finish

Plaster Finish

be consistently and perfectly covered, as with a paint application; rather, there will be some color variations. Think of an old, aged finish that has faded more in some places than in others.

To apply a colorwash, I generally use a 4-inch (10.2 cm) bristle brush and apply the glaze in back and forth or criss-cross motions. I then step back from the wall and see where the color needs to be better blended. I try to blend away the obvious brush strokes, smoothing the finish. There should be an organic feel to the overall look (not like flat paint). If you're working on a large area, you can also apply your glaze with a foam roller, then simply go back over the wall with your brush to even out the application and create the desired effect.

PLASTER

Working with plaster takes some practice. The great part about it, though, is if you don't like a particular area, you can plaster it again until you get the look you want. For this finish, I applied one coat of off-white base coat, then let it dry, and applied a thin coat of finishing plaster (or Venetian plaster), working with a trowel and a small putty knife. The plaster needs to dry at least overnight. Next, I mixed a heavy glaze at a 2:1 medium-to-tint ratio, using orange and black tint (mix the orange in first, then add drops of black one at a time to achieve a terra-cotta color). I applied the glaze over the plastered walls with a stiff bristle brush, being sure to work the glaze into the pockets and cracks; then I blended it with cheesecloth to remove obvious hard edges, and allowed it to dry. If you want a smoother plaster effect, trowel over the area a few times to smooth it out. You can also go over your plaster with a wet, closed-cell sponge. Most finishing plaster can also be sanded after it's dry to create an even smoother, softer finish.

TISSUE

To create this tissue paper finish, I first applied one coat of off-white base coat. Next, I tore white tissue into large pieces, crumpling each piece into a ball, then smoothing it back out. I then used a foam roller to roll a layer of base coat on the wall. Finally, I positioned the tissue paper on the wall and rolled over it. I repeated this process across the whole wall (overlapping paper is fine). You don't need to race the clock on this finish; if an area dries, you can still roll over it. After the finish dried (at least overnight), I made a glaze with yellow and black tints at a 4:1 medium-to-tint ratio for the yellow (with ½ part black blended in). I applied the glaze to the wall using a foam roller, then blended the wet glaze with a soft blending brush to create an overall washed effect.

This finish can also be sanded after the glaze has dried. Sanding exposes the white paper again for an aged, worn look.

REPAIRING A DECORATIVE FINISH

Because glazes are slow to dry (walls, for instance, take about 24 hours to "cure" or set), and because people don't always heed a "wet paint" sign, you may find yourself with a messed-up finish. This is not such a problem on a small project, but could be potentially a big repair on a wall.

If you end up with a handprint on a still-wet glaze, let the wall dry. Then reapply the base coat in a random pattern, on as small an area as possible, and reapply the glaze. With any luck you can blend into the adjacent areas, and the patch won't be so noticeable.

If you're not so lucky, my advice is to repaint the entire wall and glaze again. This is time-consuming and maddening, but often it's the only way to save the job. So my best advice is this: keep people and pets away from faux finishes until they're quite dry to the touch.

If you have a very small repair, say a nail hole, reapply base coats and glaze with a small artist's brush. Blend out carefully, fading into the existing finish.

Cleaning a Wall that Has a Decorative Finish

A glazed surface is usually very durable, more durable than using only house paint. You can clean glazed surfaces with water and a mild soap, but you must wait until the glaze has cured. I never wipe a glazed wall until weeks after I glaze it, and then only cautiously. After several months, the glazed surface should be fairly cleanable, but don't scrub! As with any surface treatment, a decorative finish can be worn away by things like steel wool, gritty cleaners, or harsh chemicals.

Using Color

If you've ever painted a room three different times before getting your color just right, you know that color is the most important aspect of any decorative finishing effect. Color affects the mood and energy level of a room, and consequently affects your mood and energy when you're in the room. Color can calm or excite. It can warm a room and enhance its other elements, or it can make everything in a room feel awkward and ill-fitting. Take time to learn a little about color, be confident enough to experiment, be imaginative in your use of color, and above all, look at the world around you for inspiration.

THE COLOR WHEEL

In the following section, we'll review a few fundamentals about color. You've probably learned these basics before, but take this opportunity to refresh your memory.

The *primary* colors are red, blue, and yellow—all other colors are made from these three. *Secondary* colors are created by mixing the primaries together; for example, red and blue make purple, red and yellow make orange, blue and yellow make green. *Tertiary* colors, including browns, grays, dirty purples, and earthy greens, are made by mixing a primary with a secondary color. To help you visualize how colors relate to each other, check out the color wheel (see photo, opposite page). This tool can save you lots of time and money.

Colors adjacent to each other on the color wheel are called *analogous colors.* Colors opposite each other on the wheel are called *complementary colors*, and you'll need to know about them for mixing paints and glazes, and for deciding on a color scheme. Using a complementary color scheme in a room creates a soothing and pleasant effect. Red is the opposite of green, yellow is the opposite of purple, orange is the opposite of blue, and so on. When you're mixing a glaze that turns out too blue, for instance, simply add a bit of its complement, orange, to counterbalance it. This will remove the color's harshness and "relax" it. Add complementary colors to your mix a drop or two at a time—a little goes a long way. Be careful how you use complements. If you use an orange glaze over a blue base coat, you'll get a muddy result because each color will cancel out the other. A better strategy is to "layer" colors that are similar to each other—for example, an orange glaze over a warm yellow base coat.

COLOR AND VALUE

One of the main characteristics of color is its *value*, that is, the saturation of pigment in the color. Let's say you want a cool, dark brown glaze on a wall. If you add ¼ cup (60 mL) of brown tint to ½ gallon (1.9 L) of glazing medium, you'll have mid-value glaze, that is, your color will be somewhat saturated. If you were to add 1 cup (240 mL) of tint, the value of the glaze would change significantly. The more saturated your color, the deeper, darker, thicker, and browner your glaze will be. Always start making your glazes with a small amount of tint. You can always add more, but you can't subtract.

TINTS AND SHADES

Adding white to any color creates a lighter value called a *tint*. White also adds opacity, that is, it removes the clear quality of the color and moves it toward pale or pastel.

Black is a very useful color for mixing paints and creating new colors. Adding black to any color creates a darker tone called a *shade*. Black turns yellow into olive green and orange into terra-cotta, deepening it to give it earthy tones. But beware! Add black to your paint or glaze one drop at a time. Like a complement, black has a powerful impact.

WARM AND COOL COLORS

There are warm and cool versions of every color. You can usually instinctively tell whether a color is warm or cool, but if you need a little help, think about warm colors as having more yellow tones, and cool colors having more blue tones. In the project section of this book, you'll see that some projects call for a "warm brown" glaze, as opposed to a "dark brown" one. Warm brown has a yellowish feel to it, while dark brown tends toward grayish. Warm red has an earthy yellow-to-brown quality, like a sunset or a tomato. A cool red has a blueish quality, like a bright red crayon or a pomegranate. Cool yellow is lemony, while warm yellow is moving toward gold, and so on.

You can use your color wheel to find the warm or cool versions of any color. First, find a primary color— blue, for example. When you leave blue and head toward yellow, the blue gets warmer. When you leave blue and head toward red, the blue gets cooler.

COLOR AND LIGHT

Finally, all color is affected tremendously by light. The color that looked so wonderful in the paint store may look wretched in your home. Why? The light is different. The best way to create the perfect color is to experiment and make sample boards (see page 20). Place the sample board on every wall of your room, and look at it at all times of day and night. Then you can gauge whether the value and color is right.

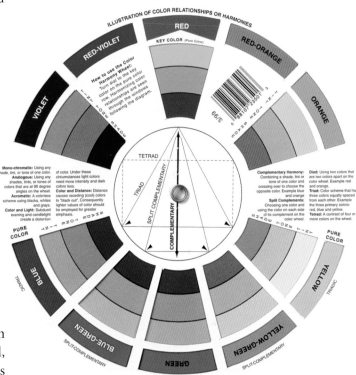

The Color Wheel Company, Philomath, Oregon

Decorative Finishes
PROJECTS

F rom flowerpots to folding screens, walls to floors, you can transform a variety of surfaces with decorative finishes that are easy to create. The projects in this section of the book will help you master basic finishes that you can apply to any surface. Try a finish on a small project first, then move on to bigger areas and surfaces. Following the simple step-by-step instructions, you'll be finishing like a pro in no time.

Tuscan Flowerpots

These aged-finish flower pots would look right at home on the steps of an Italian villa. You could spend a bundle to buy a planter with this gorgeous old-world look, or you can make one yourself with a little finishing plaster, glaze, and an ordinary terra-cotta pot. This finish also looks great on other home accents, such as ceramic bowls, vases, or candleholders.

2 Using a putty knife or even your hands (wearing gloves), apply a generous coat of finishing plaster to the outside of your pot. Smooth the surface somewhat with the putty knife, but make sure that the texture is still generally rough and uneven. Apply a layer of plaster inside the rim of the pot, starting about 2 inches (5.1 cm) down, and smooth it somewhat with your putty knife.

4 Mix a glaze (1:1 medium-to-tint ratio) using dark brown or black tint, and apply it to the surface of the pot with a stiff bristle brush, working the glaze into all the cracks.

5 Use a paper towel or rag to remove most of the glaze from the surface. Since this plaster is so sturdy, you won't need a topcoat of polyurethane.

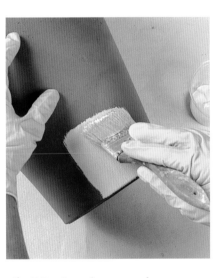

1 Wearing gloves, apply two coats of white base coat to the inside and outside of your terra-cotta pot with a 2-inch (5.1 cm) bristle brush. Allow to dry.

3 Place the pot on a piece of aluminum foil, and place it in an oven set to 175°F (79°C) until the pot is dry, about one hour. Large cracks will appear in the surface because of forced drying time. Allow the pot to cool completely.

■ IF YOU WANT MORE DEPTH OF COLOR ON YOUR POT, REPEAT STEP 4, USING ADDITIONAL TINT COLORS.

Whimsical Candleholders

When dreaming up a new decorative finish, don't limit yourself to paints. Try these versatile materials—aniline dyes and paint pens. Aniline dyes are powders that, when mixed with water, are applied like any wood stain. You can buy them in art supply or paint stores. Paint pens are easy to find at most stationery or craft supply stores. Try using them on any unfinished wood projects—a stool, chest of drawers, or even kitchen cabinets!

3 Test your colors on a scrap of wood. Observe how the stains penetrate the wood. Add more powder or water until you get the desired colors.

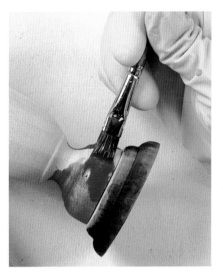

5 Apply the next color to the next section, again making sure that the colors don't bleed into each other. It's helpful to leave a small unpainted area between each color. Let each section dry for about one hour before beginning the next.

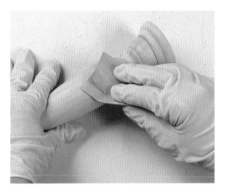

1 Sand your candleholder using 220-grit sandpaper. Remove all dust with tack cloth.

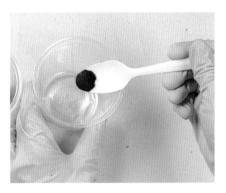

2 Mix the aniline dyes using about ¼ teaspoon (1.2 mL) powdered stain to 1 ounce (30 mL) of water. The more powder you use, the stronger your color will be.

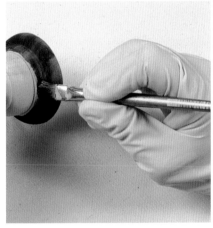

4 Using a small artist's brush, apply the first color to the base of the candleholder, being very careful not to let it seep into the next section. Stains will bleed a bit, and you don't want your colors to mix with each other. Allow the first section to dry about one hour.

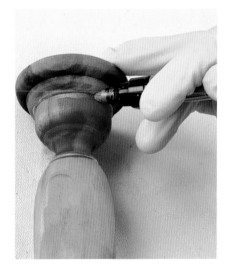

6 Using a metallic paint pen, fill in the unpainted areas and embellish with lines, stripes, dots, circles, and patterns of your own design. Seal your finish with a clear coat of polyurethane spray. Do not use brushed-on clear coat, as the colors will still bleed until sealed.

Leather-Look Tissue Paper Finish

Leather is a great look for home accessories, but it can break your budget. Achieve the same rich look of leather with a material anyone can afford —tissue paper. It's delicate to work with, and a little messy, but well worth the effort. These canisters were painted with different color base coats, but the same glaze was used for each. You can see how versatile this finish can be.

YOU WILL NEED

Cardboard or wooden canisters	Glazing medium
Disposable gloves	Dark brown tint
Base coat in desired color	Mixing bowl or tray
2-inch (5.1 cm) bristle brush	Paper towels or soft rags
White tissue paper	Small artist's brush
220-grit sandpaper	Water-based, clear polyurethane spray
Additional paint of any kind in a contrasting color for inside the canisters*	*Latex house paint or artist's acrylics work well.

1 Put on your gloves before you begin painting. Working over a protected surface, use a 2-inch (5.1 cm) bristle brush to apply the first base coat to the canister and allow it to dry.

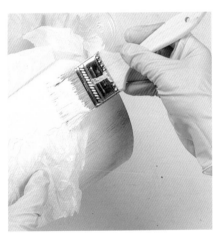

2 Tear your tissue paper into small pieces, and crumple it into a ball to give it a wrinkled texture. Load your brush with the base coat color, and paint a random patch of the canister. You don't have to coat the whole area—just make sure the surface is wet with paint. Lay a piece of tissue paper on top of the wet paint. Reload your brush and brush over the tissue, being careful not to tear the paper. Move to another section of the canister, and repeat the process until the whole surface is covered. It's okay to overlap sections; this adds dimension to the effect. Repeat the process for the canister lid.

3 While the tissue paper is still wet, tear off the excess paper at the rim of the canister and the lid. Allow the project to dry overnight.

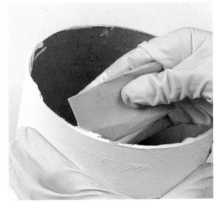

4 Sand the rim of the canister and the lid with 220-grit sandpaper to remove any rough edges. When the outside is dry, paint the inside of the canister in a contrasting color.

5 Mix a strong glaze (2:1 medium-to-tint ratio). You won't need much! Apply it with a 2-inch (5.1 cm) bristle brush, working it into all the folds.

6 With a soft paper towel or rag, remove most of the glaze. The color will adhere more strongly in the folds of the tissue paper. Allow to dry thoroughly, probably several hours.

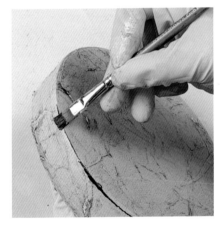

7 Using a small artist's brush, highlight the inside and outside edges of the lid and the bottom of the canister with the glaze. Let the glaze dry. Apply a spray or brush coat of polyurethane to the entire surface to seal the finish.

Distressed Copper Leaf Frame

YOU WILL NEED

Newspaper

Empty wooden frame

Low-tack painter's tape (optional)

Latex paint (optional)

Disposable gloves

Leaf adhesive*

Small artist's brush

8 to 10 copper leaf squares,* each 4 x 4 inches (10.2 x 10.2 cm)

Soft bristle brush

Cheesecloth or soft rag

Heavy-duty, chemical-resistant gloves

Old glass dish for mixing chemical solution

Water

Sodium sulfate**

Stir stick (or craft stick) for mixing solution

Small sea sponge

Garbage bag

Paper towels

Water-based, clear, spray polyurethane in a satin finish

*available at art supply stores

**available through chemical supply companies

Paints and dyes can create fascinating distressed finishes on wood or plaster, but if you're working on a metallic surface, you'll need chemicals to achieve that weather-worn look. This unusual finish is created with a chemical compound applied on top of copper leaf, but the process also works on silver, aluminum, or dutch leaf. You'll need to be extra cautious and read your manufacturer's instructions carefully when attempting this finish. Most importantly— wear chemical-resistant gloves and make sure you have proper ventilation.

NOTE: BEFORE YOU BEGIN, EITHER TAPE OFF THE GLASS OR MIRROR IN YOUR FRAME OR REMOVE IT COMPLETELY. COVER YOUR WORKSPACE WITH SEVERAL LAYERS OF NEWSPAPER. PAINT THE FRAME IF IT'S UNFINISHED OR YOU DON'T LIKE THE BASE COLOR.

1 Cover your work surface with newspapers. Wearing disposable gloves, brush the leaf adhesive onto the whole frame in even strokes. Allow the mixture to set for about 45 minutes (leaf adhesive will keep its tack for several hours).

2 Apply the copper leaf by laying it on the surface of the frame. Leave small un-leafed areas to allow the base color to show through.

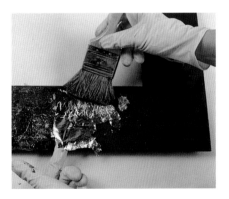

3 Brush over the leaf with a soft bristle brush.

4 Smooth over the surface with cheesecloth or a soft rag. Remove any excess leaf from the frame.

5 You must work over newspaper and wear chemical-resistant gloves for the next steps—rubber or latex gloves won't protect your hands. In an old glass dish, dissolve about 1 tablespoon (15 mL) of sodium sulfate in a small amount of water. If the granules don't completely dissolve, that's okay. They will still do the job. This solution will smell very sulfuric; make sure your workspace is well-ventilated!

6 Dab a small sea sponge into the solution, then apply the solution to the frame, leaving some areas untouched. You can also "puddle" the solution in some places for interesting effects. Allow the solution to set for several hours or overnight. When you're finished, dispose of the sponge, the solution, and the bowl by wrapping them in newspaper and placing them in a plastic garbage bag. Do **not** pour the leftover solution down your sink.

NOTE: IF THE CHEMICAL REACTION STARTS HEADING TOWARD "TOO MUCH," RINSE THE PIECE WITH WATER AND PAT IT DRY (I USE A GARDEN HOSE AND AN OLD UTILITY SINK). THAT WILL STOP THE REACTION.

7 Spray the frame with clear polyurethane, preferably in a satin finish.

Aluminum-Finish Curtain Rod

Why spend a fortune on fancy curtain rods when you can get the same elegant look from an inexpensive wooden pole and a simple decorative finish? Aluminum paint over a black base is a quick way to achieve a metallic-look curtain rod that will dress up any window treatment. If aluminum doesn't match your decor, try the same technique with a gold or copper paint. You can use this finish on any raw wood piece, from a picture frame to a chair.

3 Dip a small sea sponge into aluminum paint, and dab the sponge over the black paint in a random pattern. Don't aim for full coverage; you want a good deal of black to show through under the aluminum paint. Let the paint dry overnight.

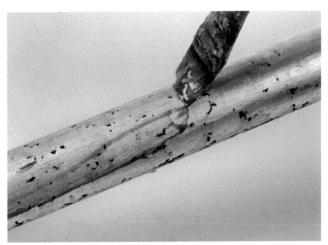

4 Mix a glaze with a raw umber (dark brown) tint using a 3:1 medium-to-tint ratio, and brush the glaze over the entire surface of the pole. Allow to dry. Spray with two coats of polyurethane to seal the finish, if desired. Attach the end finials (you can apply the same finish to the finials, paint them, or leave them as is for a contrast).

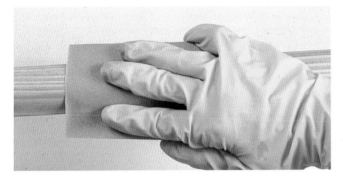

1 Sand the pole with 220-grit sandpaper; remove all dust with tack cloth.

2 Wearing gloves and working over a protected surface, use a small flat artist's brush to paint the pole with two coats of black latex paint in eggshell or semi-gloss finish. Allow to dry.

Checkerboard Combed-Finish Breakfast Tray

Combing is one of the most popular and versatile decorative finishes. It can be used to create a woodgrain effect or any number of patterns on a wall or decorative object. Dragging a comb through wet glaze creates the attractive texture. In this project, the flat bottom of the tray is painted in a checkerboard pattern, and then glazed in a different shade of blue. Once you've mastered the technique on a small project like this, try it on a wall to create a beautiful textile look.

2 Paint the inside bottom of the tray with the bright blue base coat. Use two coats. Tape off the angled interior sides of the tray if it helps you to paint more neatly. Let dry.

3 Using a straightedge (I used a paint mixing stick for this project) and a hard lead pencil or marker, draw a checkerboard pattern on the inside bottom of the tray. This tray is a 12-inch (30.5 cm) square, so I marked off 3-inch (7.6 cm) squares.

4 Mix a small amount of white base coat into your bright blue base coat to lighten it. Add enough to ensure there's a contrast between your new lighter blue color and the bright blue coat you've already painted. Paint every other square in the checkerboard pattern with your new mix of blue using a 1-inch (2.5 cm) flat artist's brush. Your coverage should look hand-painted—it doesn't have to be perfect. Let dry.

5 Mix a bright blue glaze (3:1 medium-to-tint ratio) and apply over all the squares with the artist's brush.

1 Using a 2-inch (5.1 cm) bristle brush, paint the entire tray with the warm yellow base coat. Use two coats if necessary. Let dry.

6 While the glaze is still wet, pull your rubber combing tool across each square in the manner seen in the photo.

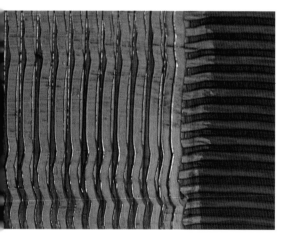

7 Alternate the pattern, using different sides of the comb to pull different patterns in adjacent squares. A vertical pull next to a horizonal pull is a nice contrast. To effectively fit the comb into corners, you can cut off some of its teeth.

8 Once the bottom of the tray is dry, mix a warm sienna glaze with a 1:1 ratio of glazing medium to tint. Starting on the angled interior sides, use the artist's brush to apply the glaze in fairly wide vertical stripes. You can measure the space in between the stripes and mark them with a pencil if you like, or paint them in a less regimented, handpainted style, as seen here. When you're finished painting the interior stripes, start painting stripes along the outside. Match them up with the interior stripes, so it looks like a continuous stripe from inside to outside.

9 When the stripes are dry, glaze the interior and exterior angled sides with a warm sienna glaze (about a 3:1 medium-to-tint ratio).

10 Paint the inside of the tray handles with a contrasting color latex paint, such as warm brown, using a small artist's brush. Spray the tray with a clear coat of polyurethane in a matte or satin finish.

Ginger Jar Lamp Revisited

You had about 10 of these lamps in the 1980s, and now they look tired and out-dated. Give your ginger jar a long-overdue facelift. For this project, you'll apply a simple sponging finish on the ginger jar. The sponge is used to dab on several layers of paint in different colors to create a mottled texture. For the shade, you'll create a coordinating strié finish using a blending brush. These are great techniques to learn on a small-scale, unintimidating project.

2 Using a small piece of a sea sponge, pick up some of the black paint or base coat and apply it to the ginger jar. Coverage should be uniform, in small specks rather than big patches.

3 Repeat step 2 with the red paint.

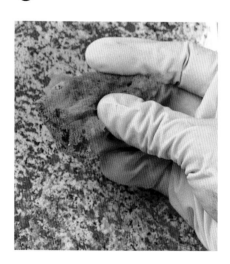

4 Repeat the same process with the light brown paint.

5 Add the dark green paint in the same manner. Use a light hand. For each additional color you add, you should still be able to distinguish the other colors.

6 Add the white paint, mixed with a touch of black, in the same way.

7 Finally, add the dark brown paint with the sea sponge. Dab a little dark brown on with the sponge, but not as much as you did with the other colors.

FOR THE GINGER JAR

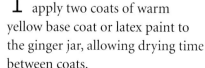

1 Using a small bristle brush, apply two coats of warm yellow base coat or latex paint to the ginger jar, allowing drying time between coats.

FOR THE SHADE

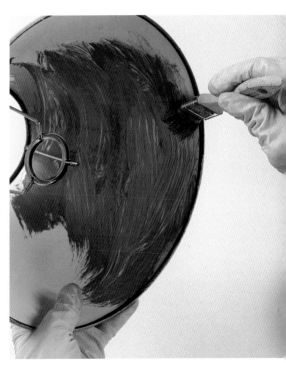

8 Mix the glazing medium and the warm sienna tint at a 1:1 ratio. Apply the glaze around the bottom edge of the shade with a bristle brush.

10 Blend the glaze with a badger brush or any very soft brush. Allow to dry.

12 Using a small brush, apply gold metallic paint to the inside of the shade. Blend or soften the look with cheesecloth, and allow to dry.

11 Use a metallic paint pen to highlight the bands of the shade.

9 Using a dry bristle brush, push the glaze up into the unglazed areas, fading the amount as you go.

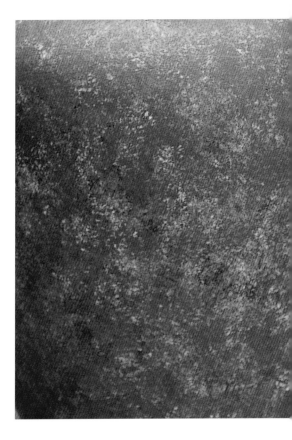

Domed Treasure Box

To store your favorite treasures, you need a box that's as special as they are. A plain unfinished wooden box can be transformed into an ancient-looking treasure chest with finishing plaster and the right paint and glaze. Since finishing plaster sticks to any surface, you don't need to worry about it bonding to your unfinished wood. Pick a rich red paint and mix up a black glaze—you'll remove a lot of it, so it won't be overwhelming. Your friends will ask where you got your stunning antique box!

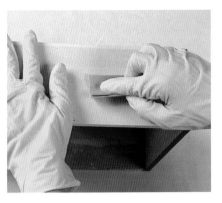

1 Remove the hardware from the box with a screwdriver. Sand any rough edges to prepare the box for painting.

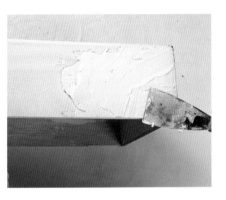

2 Apply plaster to the box and the lid using a small putty knife. Remove any plaster that gets inside the box immediately. After the plaster sets for about 10 minutes, go back over the surface with the putty knife very lightly to achieve variations in the finish.

3 Let the plaster set about 10 minutes longer, then use a pin or small nail to scratch shallow

lines in the surface. Smooth over some of the lines again with the putty knife so they look like random cracks. Allow the box to dry thoroughly. If the plaster cracks, that will only add to the effect.

4 Using your 2 to 4-inch (5.1 to 10.2 cm) bristle brush, paint the outside of the box and lid with dark reddish-orange base coat. Allow to dry.

5 Mix your glazing medium and black tint at a 1:1 medium-to-tint ratio. Apply a consistent layer of glaze to the box and lid with your bristle brush, working the glaze into all the small cracks and depressions.

6 Remove most of the glaze with a rag or cloth. Allow to dry.

7 Paint the inside of the box and lid with two coats of latex paint in a contrasting color.

8 Apply gilding cream or gold metallic paint to the edges of the box with a small artist's brush to add highlights. Apply a high-gloss polyurethane to all the interior and exterior surfaces of the box with a brush. Let the topcoat dry and reattach the hardware.

Metallic Highlight Mirror

A mirror can be an important focal point for a room, especially if you don't have much artwork on your walls. A mirror frame is a perfect place to try out new decorative finishes and add interest to a wall. This Egyptian-inspired look is easy to create, thanks to metallic paint pens. Painting directly on the mirror helps extend the decorative effect and gives you more room for creativity.

YOU WILL NEED

Mirror mounted in a wooden frame

Ruler

Soft lead pencil

High-tack painter's tape

Coin or credit card for burnishing

Black latex paint or base coat

Dark brown latex paint or base coat

Mixing bowl or tray

½-inch (1.3 cm) small, flat artist's brush

Metallic silver paint pen

Metallic gold paint pen

Water-based clear brush-on polyurethane

Single-edged razor blade

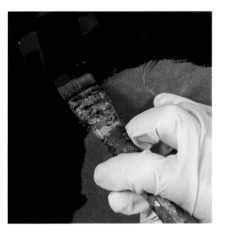

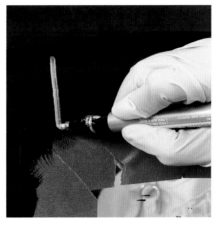

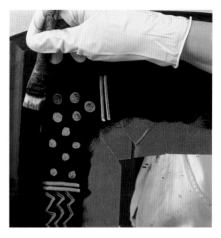

1 Measure in 2 inches (5.1 cm) from the mirror frame, and apply high-tack painter's tape all around the mirror. Burnish the edge of the tape by rubbing with a hard edge, such as a coin or credit card. This will help minimize paint seepage. Pour a small amount of the black and brown paint into a mixing bowl or tray. Using a ½-inch (1.3 cm) artist's brush, pick up some of each color and apply randomly to the entire frame and to the glass inside the tape line. *Do not* mix the brown and black; it should appear splotchy. Allow to dry.

3 Paint over the pencil lines with a metallic silver paint pen.

5 After the paint is thoroughly dry, apply two coats of clear, high-gloss polyurethane using the small, flat artist's brush.

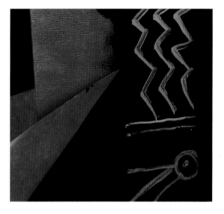

4 Create the rest of your patterns using gold and silver paint pens. You may need to pencil in the designs first. I like a symmetrical look, so I created the same designs on each side of the mirror, but reversed the orientation of the patterns.

6 Remove the tape carefully and slowly.

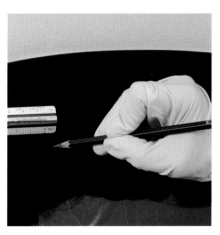

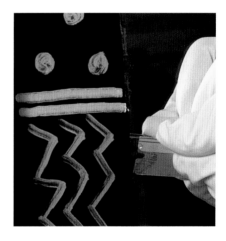

2 Decide how big each design area will be. Use a pencil to mark off each section.

7 Scrape off any seepage with a single-edged razor blade.

Animal-Print Folding Table

You don't have to be an artist or have advanced painting skills to create this wildly attractive look. The secret is all in the imprint. Imprints transfer a preprinted pattern from a coated paper to the surface of your project. All you need for the transfer is an activating liquid, called imprint medium, and a flat utensil for rubbing the back of the imprint. The result is a fantastic finish that looks like it was done by a pro.

YOU WILL NEED

TV trays or folding table,
any color or finish

Disposable gloves

Warm red base coat

White base coat

Mixing bowl or tray

4-inch (10.2 cm) polyester bristle brush

Imprints of zebra, giraffe, and ocelot*

Scissors

Small foam brush

Imprint bonding gel*

Low-tack painter's tape

Flat stick, such as a paint mixer, for
rubbing the imprint

Hard lead pencil

Drafting compass

Small artist's brush

Gold metallic pen

Glazing medium

Dark brown tint

Mixing bowl

Cheesecloth

Water-based, clear spray-on or brush-on
polyurethane in satin or matte finish

*available online from decorative
finishing sources

1 Using your 4-inch (10.2 cm) polyester bristle brush, apply two coats of warm red base coat to the legs and underside of the folding table. Paint the tabletop with a white base coat.

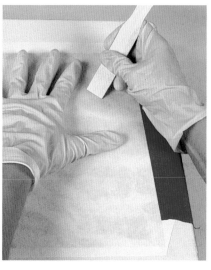

2 Cut the animal imprint to the correct size. For this project, I cut the imprint to fit on the tabletop with a 2-inch (5.1 cm) border all around. Using a foam brush, apply imprint bonding gel to the tabletop. Allow it to set for about one hour, until tacky. Place the imprint facedown on the table. Secure it to the tabletop with painter's tape. Rub the back of the imprint to transfer the color. A paint-mixing stick works well. So does a credit card!

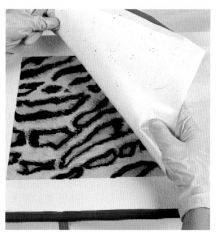

3 Carefully lift the imprint to make sure all color has been transferred. If not, place it back down and rub it again.

4 Position your drafting compass at the edge of the table, and draw a semi-circle on each corner of the imprint.

5 Paint the border of the tabletop in the same warm red you used for the rest of the table. Paint over the semicircles at each corner of the imprint in the same color. This adds interest to the border.

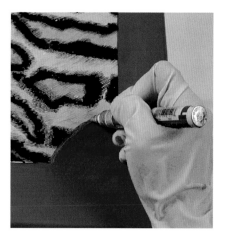

6 Highlight the border of the imprint with a gold metallic paint pen.

7 Mix a dark brown glaze (3:1 medium-to-tint ratio), and apply it to the entire table.

8 While it's still wet, blend the glaze with cheesecloth, removing some glaze. Allow the piece to dry overnight. Apply two coats of clear polyurethane in a satin or matte finish to the top of the table. Use more clear coat if the table will get a lot of use.

Crackle Finish Dustbin

No decorative painting book would be complete without a crackle-finish project. It's one of the most popular finishes around, seen on everything from blanket chests to doors and window frames. But using a crackle medium can be tricky! I created this project using random crackling patterns, making the application a little easier. A big unfinished wooden box like this can be used for many purposes, including hiding your trash. Practice using crackle medium on a small project like this before trying it on a big project like a wall.

YOU WILL NEED

Lidded wooden box or hamper

Lightweight hole filler

Putty knife

220-grit sandpaper

Power sander (optional)

Mixing tray or bowl

Light brown flat latex paint

Black flat latex paint

4-inch (10.2 cm) synthetic brush

Crackle medium*

Gray base coat

Water

Glazing medium

Raw umber or black tint

Cheesecloth

Orange tint

½-inch (1.3 cm) flat artist's brush

Mahogany-tinted furniture wax

Clean soft cloths

Water-based, clear, brush-on
polyurethane in any finish

*available at paint, craft, or home
improvement stores

1 Fill any rough-cut edges on the box with lightweight hole filler. Smooth the hole filler on with a putty knife, and allow to dry. Sand the surface of the box with 220-grit sandpaper. Pour light brown and black flat latex paint onto your mixing tray, but do **not** mix yet. Load your 4-inch (10.2 cm) bristle brush with paint in each color, and roughly and randomly paint the entire box, starting with the lid. You do **not** need full or perfect coverage. Allow to dry.

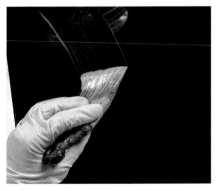

2 With a clean brush, apply the crackle medium evenly over the entire piece, being careful not to leave drips or bare spots. Allow the crackle medium to dry for about one hour (it should feel completely dry to the touch).

3 Thin the gray base coat with water until it has a very light, fluid consistency. With your brush, apply the base coat to the box in random, crisscross strokes. As soon as this coat is applied, the crackling will begin. You **cannot** brush back over a painted area once crackles appear, so you have to work fast. This is why you want your paint to be thin enough to be spread on quickly. This coat will not look even.

4 Once this coat has dried you should see a random crackle pattern, but it will look a little blotchy. Make a wash using gray base coat and water in a 1:1 ratio. Apply over the entire piece. This should even out the overall color. Allow to dry, preferably overnight.

5 Make a glaze using raw umber (dark brown) or black tint at a 1:1 medium-to-tint ratio. Brush the glaze over the entire box.

6 Fold your cheesecloth into a pad, and dab or rub the glaze to create streaks and darker areas. Bear in mind that furniture does not age uniformly. It's supposed to look like it's been sitting in the attic for 100 years!

7 Mix a strong orange glaze (1:10 medium-to-tint ratio). Outline the edges of the box with glaze using a ½-inch (1.3 cm) flat artist's brush. Allow to dry.

8 With a soft cloth, apply two coats of tinted furniture wax (I used antique mahogany), and buff with another clean, soft cloth after each coat. Finish with several coats of clear polyurethane brushed inside the box (the wax is enough to protect the outside), allowing drying time between coats.

Antiqued Chest of Drawers

Can't find the perfect antique dresser you've been looking for? Why not paint a new unfinished piece to match your decor? You can create an antique effect with a very simple glaze and some highlighting. Gold metallic paint is the key to this look. Handpainted lines add to the charm of this piece, so don't worry if your lines aren't perfect.

2 Go over each area with very light brush strokes—vertical on the sides, horizontal on the top and drawer fronts. Allow to dry overnight.

3 Brush a layer of clear polyurethane inside the drawers, and allow to dry.

4 Using a ¼-inch (6 mm) flat artist's brush and water-based gold paint, paint borders around the drawers, top, sides, and front of the dresser. The look should be "freehand." On longer sides, you may attach painter's tape to give you a straighter edge. Remove the tape immediately after painting, and touch up any errors.

1 Sand the entire piece with 220-grit sandpaper (inside and out), and apply two coats of off-white base coat to all outer surfaces with the 4-inch (10.2 cm) bristle brush. Smooth out your brush strokes by lightly brushing the surface after you apply the paint. Sand lightly between coats. Allow to dry, then mix and apply a light green glaze (2:1 medium-to-green tint ratio, plus a drop of dark brown). Apply the glaze to the chest, working one section at a time.

5 Apply another glaze using green only (1:1 medium-to-tint ratio—the same as in step 1, but without the brown). Allow to dry. Brush on two coats of clear polyurethane, allowing 30 minutes drying time between coats. If the dresser is going to get rough wear, you may want to put three to four coats on the chest top. Reattach your hardware

Venetian Plaster Wall Finish

This project uses the same material as the Domed Treasure Box (pages 44-45) and the Tuscan Flowerpots (pages 28-29), but on a much larger, more ambitious scale. If you've never plastered a wall, you might want to practice in a small area before tackling a whole room. Once you've got the hang of it, try creating this worn, aged look in a kitchen or bathroom.

YOU WILL NEED

Low-tack painter's tape

Drop cloths

Disposable gloves

Off-white base coat

10-inch (25.4 cm) foam roller

Roller pan or tray

Finishing plaster*

Putty knife

10-inch (25.4 cm) plastering trowel

Bucket of hot water

Synthetic closed-celled sponge

Glazing medium

Orange tint

Dark brown tint

Black tint

4-inch (10.2 cm) synthetic brush

Soft rags or paper towels (optional)

Utility knife

*Finishing plaster is available through decorative finishing sources or home improvement stores. It's sold by the gallon. Each gallon covers approximately 300 square feet (27m²).

1 Tape off ceiling, windows, doors, and baseboards and put down drop cloths. Apply two coats of the off-white base coat, allowing two to three hours drying time between coats.

4 If you prefer a smoother look, wet the closed-cell sponge and skim over the plaster while the plaster is still somewhat wet (within 15 minutes of application). Allow the walls to dry overnight.

6 Apply the glaze to the walls using the 4-inch (10.2 cm) synthetic brush. Work the glaze into the cracks and depressions created by the plaster. Distribute the glaze over the walls with the brush in a random fashion, criss-crossing your strokes.

2 Use the putty knife to load the trowel with plaster.

5 Prepare a glaze using orange and dark brown tint. For a terra cotta effect, mix a 3:1 medium-to-tint ratio with the orange tint, and add about ½ of one part black.

3 Using the trowel, skim across the wall, making several passes until you get the look you want. The plaster should vary in thickness. Leave some places unplastered. For tight corners, use your putty knife as a trowel. Wipe any plaster off trim or baseboards immediately.

7 Brush over the same areas again and again, removing hard brush strokes and creating a washed look. You may wish to remove some of the glaze using a soft cloth. You want to achieve a washed and worn look, not a uniform color throughout. Allow to dry. Remove the tape by cutting through the finish to the tape with a utility knife and then lifting off the tape. Do not simply pull the tape off, as that will pull the plaster off the wall as well.

Harlequin *Faux Bois* Floor

Beautiful wood floors can make a room, but what do you do if your floors have lost their luster? Try this wood-look finish, called faux bois, and a harlequin or diamond-shaped pattern. It's perfect for hiding flaws and imperfections in a wooden floor, drawing attention away from defects in the wood, and focusing it on the bigger picture—the diamond-shaped pattern. The warm brown glaze mimics a real wood finish—only the most discerning eye will be able to tell the difference.

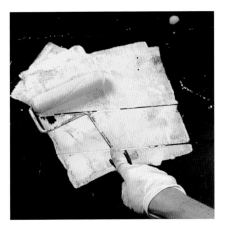

1 Vacuum and clean your floor with a trisodium phosphate substitute, and let it dry. Wearing disposable gloves, apply two or three coats of warm yellow base coat to the floor with a roller, and let it dry.

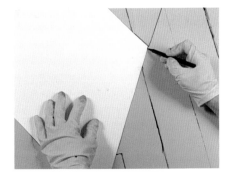

2 Photocopy the harlequin template on page 73, and enlarge it to the desired size for your floor pattern (the pattern for this project was approximately 2 ½-feet long x 12 inches wide (76.2 x 30.5 cm). Copy the template onto cardboard or stiff poster paper. Find the center point of two adjoining walls in your room. Using a straightedge and a pencil, draw a line from each wall to this point. This is the center against which you line up your first row of diamonds. Set your template on the floor with the center of the diamond over the center point. Trace around it with a soft pencil. Move the top point of the template to the bottom point of the drawn diamond, and trace another diamond. Continue this process going down the floor and then across until the pattern extends across the whole floor.

3 Mix a glaze using dark brown, warm brown, and a touch of red, to suit your desired outcome. Using a 4-inch (10.2 cm) stiff

bristle brush, apply the glaze to every other diamond, moving from the left to the right, from the top to the bottom of the floor. Apply the glaze in straight stokes to achieve a natural wood-grain look. Allow to dry overnight.

4 Add a little more color to the glaze you created in step 3. Using a soft bristle brush, apply the glaze across the entire floor, over the diamonds that are already glazed and those that are unglazed. Again, pull down in straight lines to create a strié (striped) effect that resembles wood graining. Allow to dry overnight.

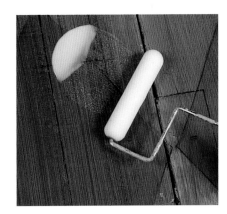

5 Apply several coats of satin water-based polyurethane topcoat across the whole floor with a roller.

Aged Chinese Newspaper Wall Finish

Chinese characters have a simple graphic quality that looks impressive even if you don't understand their meaning. On a wall, Chinese newspapers can create a striking pattern.

Use them like wallpaper to camouflage a dull or damaged section of the wall.

You can also use this finish on small decorative items, such as boxes, canisters, or trays.

Once you've mastered this technique, you can turn any paper into distinctive wallpaper.

YOU WILL NEED

Disposable gloves

Water-based, clear, brush-on polyurethane in satin or high-gloss finish

10-inch (25.4 cm) foam roller

Chinese newspapers

Glazing medium

Dark brown tint

Mixing pan or bowl

4-inch (10.2 cm) bristle brush

Badger blending brush

2 Repeat the process until the entire wall is covered. It's okay to overlap the pieces in a random pattern. Allow to dry overnight.

4 Mix a glaze using dark brown tint, adding tint until you reach the depth of color you want (a light orange glaze also looks good on Chinese newspaper). Apply the glaze using a 4-inch (10.2 cm) bristle brush.

1 Using a foam roller and clear polyurethane base coat, paint a section of your wall. Place a sheet of Chinese newspaper on top of the wet clear coat, and roll over it until it's thoroughly soaked and adhered firmly to the wall. (Briefly soak the newspaper first so it's damp, not wet; if you apply it to the wall dry, it will wrinkle.)

3 As the newspaper dries, add more clear coat if there are places where the paper didn't adhere, and let these additional coats dry.

5 Use a badger brush to smooth the brush strokes. Let dry. If you want, apply another coat of polyurethane for durability, using your roller to create even coverage and avoid brush strokes.

Sueded Wall Finish

A suede finish is a subtle, sophisticated way to add interest to your walls (it's also great for home accents). For this "bagging" technique, thin plastic grocery bags are used to manipulate the glaze, creating a soft texture. The trick is to work over the same areas of your wall with the bag several times. The more you manipulate the glaze, the more refined the finish becomes.

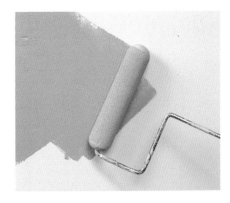

2 Begin cutting in with a bristle brush; then use a foam roller to paint the rest of the walls with the grey-green base coat. Apply two coats of base coat, allowing three to four hours drying time between coats. Allow the wall to dry overnight after the final coat.

4 Crumple up your plastic bag until it's about the size of a grapefruit. While the glaze is very wet, dab the bag into the glaze, and pat or tap the wall with it to break up the roller or brush strokes. Be sure to get into the edges and corners with the bag. Make sure you don't apply the glaze too thickly, or it will be difficult to remove later. Keep a wet, unworked edge as you go. Work fast. Step back from your wall from time to time to check for missed spots.

1 Prep and patch walls as necessary, or take advantage of small flaws in your wall and let them become part of the finish. Tape off the ceiling, baseboards, windows, and doorways with low-tack painter's tape.

3 Make a glaze using dark brown and warm brown tints (3:1 medium-to-tint ratio). You're going for a warm, amber-look glaze. Apply the glaze to the entire wall in a random pattern with crisscrossing strokes, using the 4-inch (10.2 cm) brush. If you have a huge surface to cover, use a roller to apply the glaze.

5 A few minutes after the first bagging, the glaze will be thinner and more resistant. For the best results, a second person should start bagging over the first manipulation about 10 minutes after the first person started.Repeat this process if you want a finer texture.

Tone-on-Tone Striped Wall

Vertical stripes add an air of elegance to a wall. You can actually achieve this finish two ways—by using paint in two finishes, such as matte and satin or semi-gloss and gloss, or by starting with flat wall paint and adding a stripe of clear topcoat, as I did for the wall in this project. Either way, it's a very simple way to dress up a room without the mess, fuss, and permanence of wallpaper.

1 Patch and prep your walls as needed. Tape off your ceiling, trim, and baseboards with low-tack painter's tape, and begin cutting in with a bristle brush. Cover the entire wall with two coats of your first color or finish (in this case, the flat latex paint). Allow the paint to cure for at least 24 hours, or more if the weather is humid.

2 Determine how wide your stripes will be. For this project, they were 6 inches (15.2 cm) wide. At the top of the wall, make small hash marks with a hard lead pencil every 6 inches (15.2 cm) around the entire room. Begin in the most inconspicuous corner of the room—the corner that gets the very least attention. This is where your stripes will end and where you'll be aligning the pattern.

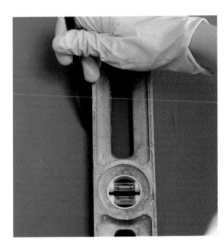

3 Using a 4-foot (1.2 m) level and a hard lead pencil, draw your vertical stripes, beginning at the hash marks at the top, coming down from the trim. Hold your level to the wall and center the bubble. Draw down a 4-foot (1.2 m)

line, using the line just drawn to situate the next one. Center the bubble again. Continue repositioning the level and drawing the vertical lines down the wall until you reach the baseboard or floor.

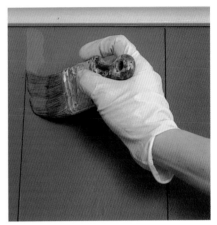

4 With a 2-inch (5.1 cm) angled trim brush, paint alternating stripes in the clear topcoat or second color. Again, start from your most inconspicuous corner and work your way around the room. Your stripes don't have to be perfect. In fact, a little irregularity only adds to the effect. If there's not enough contrast when you're finished, your stripes may need a second coat, but in most cases this is unnecessary.

Simple Colorwash Wall
with Antiqued Embossed Border

A colorwash is one of the simplest and most attractive wall finishes around. It can add texture and depth to a wall without overwhelming the surroundings, and it's easy to do. Add a wallpaper border to a wall that's been antiqued with glaze, and you've got an elegant look for any room in the house.

YOU WILL NEED

Disposable gloves

Low-tack painter's tape

Base coat in warm yellow

Roller pan

Foam roller

4-inch (10.2 cm) bristle brush

Glazing medium

Mixing bowl or tray

Orange tint

Dark brown tint

Black tint

Cheesecloth

1- to 2-inch (2.5 to 5.1 cm) bristle brush

Badger blending brush

Prepasted embossed wallpaper border

Rag or paper towel

Tape measure

Hard lead pencil

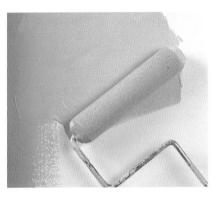

1 Prep and patch your walls as needed, and tape off your ceiling, windows, doors, and baseboards. Apply two coats of the warm yellow base coat: first, cut in around the trim, using a roller or brush as needed, then paint the rest of the surface. Allow three to four hours drying time between coats. After the second coat, allow the wall to cure overnight.

2 Mix a glaze with orange tint mixed at about a 3:1 medium-to-tint ratio. Add dark brown tint and a touch of black. Add the black tint a drop at a time, mixing well after each addition. Keep going until you achieve the depth of color you want—you're going for a rich terra-cotta.

3 Apply the glaze to the wall using a 4-inch (10.2 cm) brush or foam roller. Always leave a wet, unworked edge.

4 Gather the cheesecloth into a ball, folding all the raw edges under so stray threads won't land in the glaze. Softly dab the walls with the cheesecloth, turning your cloth back and forth like a pendulum as you work. Your application should be random, not even.

5 Brush over the entire surface of the wall with a badger blending brush to soften the texture. Softly blend the finish, moving the brush up and down, back and forth.

6 Mix a dark brown glaze using a 1:1 medium-to-tint ratio. Apply the glaze to your embossed wallpaper border with a 1 to 2-inch (2.5 to 5.1 cm) bristle brush.

7 Use a rag or paper towel to remove most of the glaze from the border.

8 Measure and mark on your wall the horizontal line that you'll use as the top of your border. Measure and mark the height of your border (it can be used as a chair rail or wall border). Hang the border according to the manufacturer's instructions.

African Mudcloth Floorcloth

The striking, simple patterns of African mudcloth are recreated in this functional painted floorcloth. Painted to echo the warm, handloomed texture of real mudcloth, this floorcloth adds interest to a floor without tying you down to a permanent paint job. You don't need stencils or templates for this one—you can mark off different sections with just a pencil and ruler. The designs are done freehand, so you can paint as loosely as you like. If you're using this floorcloth over a bare floor in a high traffic area, buy a very thin rug pad to use underneath.

YOU WILL NEED

Preprimed canvas measuring 46 x 64 inches
(116.8 x 162.5 cm)

White latex house paint or artist's acrylic paint

Roller pan

4-inch (10.2 cm) foam roller

Duct tape or two-sided carpet tape

Soft lead pencil

Tape measure

3-foot (91.4 cm) straightedge

Disposable gloves

Black flat latex paint

2-inch (5.1 cm) angled synthetic brush

1-inch (2.5 cm) flat artist's brush

Gold metallic paint pen

Mixing tray or bowl

Glazing medium

Dark brown tint

4-inch (10.2 cm) stiff bristle brush

Cheesecloth

Water-based clear polyurethane finish

2 Create a checkerboard pattern on your canvas by drawing a series of 9-inch (22.9 cm) squares inside the rectangle. The easiest way to do this is to set your tape measure along each edge, and mark every 9 inches (22.9 cm). Connect the hash marks using a straight-edge.

3 With the 2-inch (5.1 cm) angled brush, paint the outside border and every other square with the black paint. One coat should be enough. Use your pencil marks as guidelines only. You don't need to paint perfect squares—you're striving for a hand-painted fabric effect. Erase any unwanted pencil marks after the black paint has dried.

1 Paint your canvas with the white latex paint using a roller or a brush. Let dry. Hem it by turning under 2 inches (5.1 cm) on all four sides and taping the hem to the back with duct tape or two-sided carpet tape. Your canvas will now measure 42 x 60 inches (106.7 x 152.4 cm). Measure and mark a 3-inch (7.6 cm) border on all four sides of the canvas. You should now have rectangle that measures 36 x 54 inches (91.4 x 137.2 cm).

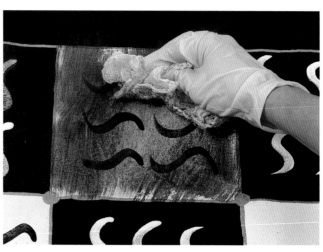

4 Using a 1-inch (2.5 cm) flat artist's brush, paint a white, freestyle wavy design on each black square. Repeat this design on the white squares using black paint.

7 With cheesecloth, dab the surface, softening and blending the glaze. Continue to dab with cheese-cloth until you've removed a lot of the glaze and have a achieved a soft effect. Allow to dry.

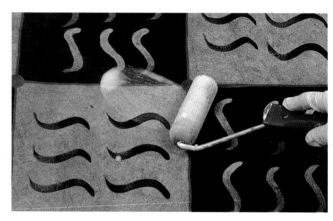

5 Outline each square with a gold paint pen. Again, imperfections are good. Draw circles at the intersections of the squares.

8 Using the foam roller, coat the floorcloth with a clear acrylic finish. Apply at least two coats, using more if the floorcloth will be used in a high traffic area, such as a bathroom.

6 Let dry. Mix a dark brown glaze (1:1 medium-to-tint ratio.) Brush the glaze over each square with a 4-inch (10.2 cm) bristle brush.

Moroccan Souk Folding Screen

Folding screens are great for dividing a space or hiding a room's less attractive features, but many of them come with plain, dull canvas panels. Why not use the blank canvas to create an evocative decorative finish? Using simple stencils and templates, you can create an exotic Moroccan mood for your room. This project is a great solution when you don't want to commit to a permanent wall finish—when you're ready for a change, just pick up your screen and move it, or paint another finish over it.

2 Using the roller, apply the paint to the screen's canvas panels in a random pattern. Move the roller back and forth, mixing the two colors together. Paint the front of each panel in the screen to about two-thirds of the way down the screen, leaving the bottom third of the screen unpainted. You don't have to paint the panels evenly—the irregularities in the color are part of the appeal of this finish. Allow to dry.

3 Tape your stencil in place at the top of the first canvas panel. Using the foam roller, paint over the stencil with the yellow-gold paint. Don't overload the roller, or paint will seep under the stencil—use a light touch.

1 Pour a small amount of dark blue and light blue paint into a mixing tray or plate. Your pools of paint should be near enough to each other to touch without mixing too much. Using a small foam roller, pick up some of both colors on opposite sides of the roller.

4 Reposition the stencil and repeat step 3 until you've stenciled over the whole painted surface. Repeat the whole process for each panel in the screen. Let dry.

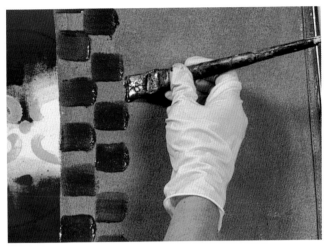

6 Using a flat 1-inch (2.5 cm) artist's brush, paint the square bottom portion of the minaret with gold water-based paint. When the gold paint is dry, paint a checkerboard pattern over it using bronze water-based paint and a ½-inch (1.3 cm) flat artist's brush.

5 Photocopy the minaret template on page 73, enlarging it to fit inside the unpainted bottom third of the canvas panel (or make your own template). Copy the template onto heavy poster board or cardboard. Cut out the template and place it on the canvas with the onion dome facing upward (the minaret should overlap into the painted and stenciled portion of the screen). Tape the stencil in place if you need to. Trace around the template with a marker.

7 For the middle section of the minaret, apply the same warm yellow-gold paint you used to create the stencil pattern.

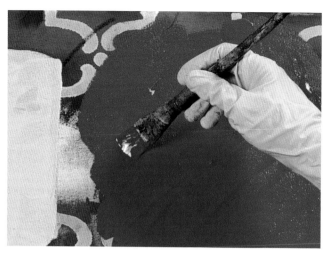

8 Paint the onion dome warm red with a ½-inch (1.3 cm) flat artist's brush.

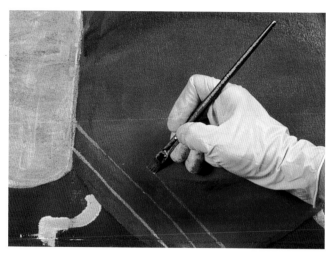

11 Using the small, flat artist's brush, paint diagonal lines across the onion dome in gold metallic paint. Outline entire minaret in gold, if you wish.

9 Mix a brown glaze (1:1 medium-to-tint ratio), and apply it to the yellow-gold middle section of the minaret with a ½-inch (1.3 cm) flat artist's brush.

10 Apply the glaze you mixed in step 9 to the outer edges of the onion dome.

Templates

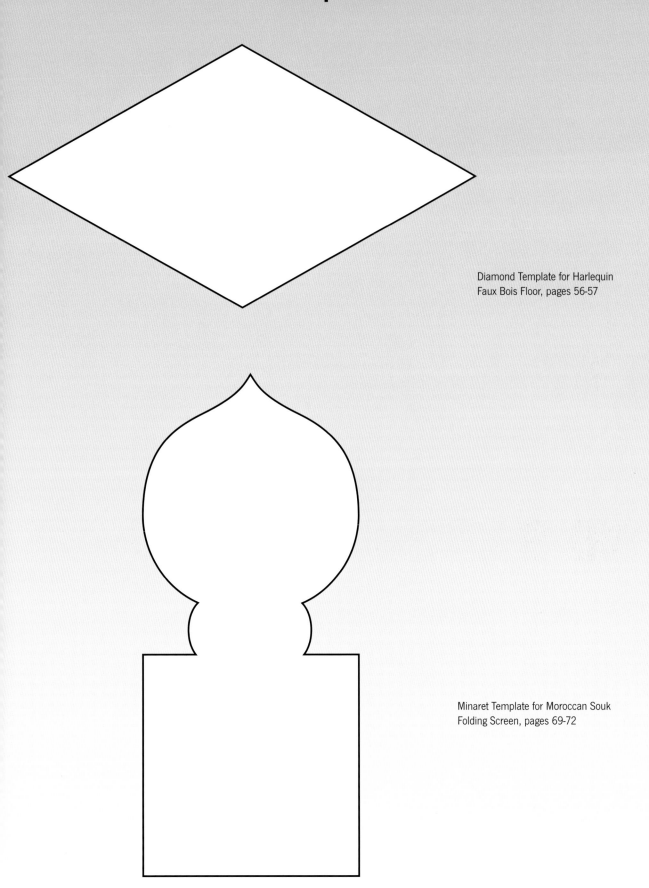

Diamond Template for Harlequin
Faux Bois Floor, pages 56-57

Minaret Template for Moroccan Souk
Folding Screen, pages 69-72

Gallery

Randy Davidson, Stamped leather bathroom wall fir
carmel colored base coat with multiple applications o
paint-glaze mix, rolled on and ragged off, stamped wi
2:1 glaze mixture, dull varnish top coat. PHOTO BY ARTIS

Randy Davidson, Strié wall finish: acorn latex glaze mixed with water and brushed over mustard yellow base coat. PHOTO BY ARTIST

Randy Davidson, Red leather wall finish: red base coat sponged with three layers of paint-glaze mix. Photo by artist

Derick Tickle, Lyna Farkas, Spirit of Decorum, Linen wall finish: Pink latex glaze brushed in opposite directions over white, satin-sheen, latex base coat with a strié brush. Photo by Derick Tickle

Lyna Farkas, Spirit of Decorum. Strié finish. Photo by artist

Derick Tickle, Lyna Farkas, Two-tone sponged wall finish: Mocha glaze, muted with natural sea sponge, softened with cheesecloth over off-white base coat. Photo by Derick Tickle

Derick Tickle, Porch stencil: pat[...]
paint over deck paint finish, hand[...]
stencils from mylar, applied with f[...]
stencil brushes. PHOTO BY DERICK T[...]

Sheila Ennis, Metallic color wash over gray base coat.

Lyna Farkas, Red leather wall finish: burgundy latex glaze sponged over bright red base coat, softened with cheesecloth. PHOTO BY DERICK TICKLE

Decorative Restoration Program, AB-Tech, Asheville North Carolina, Rag-rolled walls: light tan glaze applied over white walls with loosely rolled damp rags.
PHOTO BY DERICK TICKLE

Tom Shulz, Highlighted decorative finish mirror.

Sheila Ennis, Marbled finish buffet top.

Glossary

Angled or angular brush. A flat brush with bristles that are cut at an angle to make getting into corners easier.

Badger blending brush. A specialty decorative painting brush made from soft badger hair. Used for a final touch to blend brush strokes from a glaze.

Bagging. Manipulating a wet glaze with a plastic bag. See also ragging and padded finish.

Base coat. The first coat of paint applied in a finish. A glaze is applied over a base coat.

Blending. A soft or gradual transition from one color or tone to another. Also, a softening technique to reduce brushstrokes.

Burnishing. Rubbing vigorously to smooth a surface or transfer an image.

Cheesecloth. A lightweight cotton gauze material used to manipulate glazes.

Clear coat. See topcoat.

Colorwashing. A translucent "washed" effect achieved when a thin glaze is brushed over a painted surface, then blended with a brush or cloth"

Combing. Using a rubber comb, dragged across a just-painted surface to create stripes, plaids, waves, or squares.

Crackle medium. An antiquing medium used between two layers of paint. The top paint layer reacts with the crackle glaze and forms cracks, revealing the base color to create an aged paint look.

Curing time. The amount of time it takes for paint to "set," or reach its most stable state.

Cutting in. Applying paint around doors, ceilings, and trim carefully before applying it to a whole wall.

Distressing. Any technique that simulates the effects of wear and tear on newly painted surfaces.

Dragging. Using a paintbrush pulled in a straight "drag" across a wet surface to create a grained effect. See also strié.

Drybrushing. See blending.

Eggshell finish. See satin finish.

Faux finish. Decorative painting that imitates the look of wood, marble, etc. Faux means false.

Finishing coat. See topcoat.

Finishing plaster. See also Venetian plaster. A recently developed plaster product that can be applied to almost any surface to create a textured look.

Flat brush. A brush with squared-off bristles with a sharp edge.

Glazing. Applying glaze to a previously painted area.

Glazing medium. Transparent liquid that's combined with paint or tint to create a glaze that is then manipulated to create a decorative finish.

Gloss finish. Shiny finish with a reflective quality.

Graining. See Dragging

Hole filler. Lightweight plasterlike product used to patch holes in preparation for painting.

Imprint bonding agent. Liquid used to activate the transfer of an image from a specially-treated paper to a surface.

Matte finish. Flat finish with no gloss.

Open time. The period of time when a glaze is still wet and easy to manipulate.

Padded finish. See also bagging and ragging.

Pouncing. Giving a textured appearance by lightly loading a small amount of paint onto a brush and "pouncing" up and down on the painted surface, allowing some background color to show through.

Primer. A product designed to go under a coat of paint to prepare a surface to accept paint.

Ragging. Giving a textured effect by bouncing or dabbing a rag up and down on freshly applied glaze. See also bagging and padded finish.

Random edge. Glaze applied not in squares, but in loose organic patterns.

Rubber comb. A toothed implement developed for woodgraining and now used for other decorative finishing techniques.

Satin finish. Finish with a light gloss.

Semi-gloss finish. Somewhat shiny, durable finish.

Sponging. Using sea sponges to apply or remove paint from a surface.

Strié. A dragged paint or woodgrain finish.

Softening. See blending.

Tack cloth. Cheesecloth treated with a sticky substance so that it collects and traps dust and dirt.

Topcoat. Clear coat of varnish or polyurethane applied after a glaze to protect a finish from scuffing or chipping.

Undercoat. See base coat. Preliminary color over which other colors or glazes are applied.

Universal tints. Highly concentrated liquid pigment for coloring oil or water- based paints. Used by professional house painters and decorative painters.

Venetian plaster. A recently developed plaster product that can be applied to almost any surface to create a textured look.

Wet edge. Keeping a portion of a glaze unmanipulated and wet so that there is a gradual, rather than a harsh, transition between areas of glaze application.

Acknowledgments

It takes many people to put a book together. I would like to thank the folks whose hard work made this book both possible and fun.

To a great friend and editor, Deborah Morgenthal, thanks for the chance. Thank you also to Carol Taylor, tireless publisher. I appreciate the people at Lark Books who made it possible to photograph the projects in Boston. That couldn't have been easy! Of course, I can't forget the fine photographer Evan Bracken who made a week of work a week of fun...thanks Evan. To my best buddy Kevin McPheeters, many thanks for your artistic input and for helping me pull things together at the very last minute. My most humble and gracious thanks to Melinda Ashley and Michelle Ashley, extraordinary artists who allowed us to raid their lofts for props. What great sports you are. Thanks to Jane Wolfe for about a million things, including the use of her apartment. And to one amazing editor, Joanne O'Sullivan, who never got mad when I forgot things and who kept me focused and for the most part meeting the deadlines. She also does great rewrites and can make sense of almost anything. It was great fun working with all of you.

And to Tom Schulz, a special thank you—not only for giving up your studio for a week—but for building all those "rooms" that made our work so easy. And, or course, for enabling me to do this at all...love and thanks.

Gallery Artists

Derick Tickle trained in England as an apprentice and serves as an examiner and advisor for the City and Guilds of London in Decorative Painting. He has facilitated workshops and seminars for TV set designers, interior decorators, and professionals in the UK, New Zealand, and USA. He currently teaches Decorative Painting and Restoration at Asheville-Buncombe Technical College in Asheville, North Carolina, USA, www.asheville.cc.nc.us.

Lyna Farkas is a graduate of the Decorative Painting and Restoration Program at Asheville-Buncombe Technical College. She designs and paints professionally through her business: Spirit of Decorum in Asheville, North Carolina, USA, e-mail: fauxluv@aol.com.

Randy Davidson experimented with decorative painting in his own home, and then went on to study techniques through workshops and classes in Dallas, Texas. He now works full-time with homebuilders on decorative painting and design contracts through his business: Shamrock Homes "In the Faux," Little Rock, Arkansas, USA.

Tom Schulz received his MFA from Tufts University and the School of Museum of Fine Art, Boston. He is an adjunct faculty member with the School of Museum of Fine Art (SMFA) and a visual artist. He's also interested in performance art and does artistic installations in concrete.

Index